Woman
To
Woman

Woman To Woman

Candid Conversations From Me to You

JOYCE MEYER

NEW YORK BOSTON NASHVILLE

FaithWords
Hachette Book Group USA
237 Park Avenue, New York, NY 10017
Visit our Web site at www.faithwords.com.

Printed in the United States of America

First FaithWords Edition: January 2007
10 9 8 7 6 5 4 3

FaithWords is a division of Hachette Book Group USA, Inc.
The FaithWords name and logo is a trademark of Hachette Book Group USA, Inc.

ISBN 978-0-446-58181-3 (Special Sales Edition)

Contents

Contents

Introduction

As a busy woman in today's fast-paced, high-pressure world, I'm sure that you know about the frustration that comes from all the demands on your time. Sometimes it seems that life gets unorganized and out of control in spite of your best efforts to properly prioritize your activities and manage your time. The challenges of career, finances, marriage, raising children, and other urgent demands limit your personal privacy and crowd out your quality time with God.

I know because I've been there. I may look like I have it all together today when I step on the platform to minister to others, but you should have seen what I was like during the years while God was preparing me for the ministry. I lived with frustration and pressure, experiencing all the same challenges that you may be dealing with right now.

Then God gave me revelation about the unique woman He had created me to be. He assured me that the Holy Spirit was walking alongside me, transforming me into an anointed and effective woman of God who is equipped to make a difference for the kingdom of heaven.

If you are struggling with the myriad challenges that you face in today's busy world and feel that you are not as far along in becoming the godly woman you want to be, don't despair. God isn't through with you yet. He wants you to realize that you are a unique woman, and that He has a unique plan for your life.

A good way to discover this plan is by starting each day by declaring, "This is the day the Lord has made. [I] will rejoice and be glad in it" (Psalm 118:24 NLT). Then spend some intimate time with the Lord, focusing on Him and renewing your commitment to seek and follow His will.

What I have experienced and enjoyed will work for you too. I believe the heartwarming stories I share in these pages will help you remember that the Holy Spirit is walking alongside you each day, helping you to accomplish God's will for your life.

You must always remember that you are a rare, one-of-a-kind, valuable woman of God with a unique sphere of influence. God wants to bring you freedom from the daily frustrations and challenges of being a woman and help you become all that you can be. Then He wants to empower you to use your unique abilities to share His love in your little corner of the world.

Woman
to
Woman

1

Looking for Contentment in All the Wrong Places

Women of God should be peaceful, joyful, thankful, and content. In Philippians 4:11, Paul said that he had "learned how to be content." Well, I don't know about you, but I spent many years, even as a believer, before I learned contentment, and I believe there are many other women who struggle as I did trying to find it. You may be one of them.

I knew how to be satisfied if I was getting my own way—if everything was working exactly as I had planned, but how often does that happen? Very rarely, in my experience. I knew absolutely nothing about how to handle even the ordinary trials that come along in most every woman's life. I didn't know how to adapt to other people and things.

I found out that a woman who can only be satisfied when there are no disturbances in life will spend much of her time being discontented. I finally desired stability enough that I was willing to learn whatever it took to have it. I wanted to be *satisfied* no matter what was going on around me.

The Amplified Bible defines the word *content* as "(satisfied to the point where I am not disturbed or disquieted) in whatever state I am in" (v. 11). I appreciate this definition because it does not say that I must be satisfied to the point where I don't ever want change, but I can be satisfied to the point that I am not anxious or disturbed. I desperately wanted and now enjoy that kind of peace. How about you?

I am going to share with you four things that I think lead to feelings of discontentment, especially among women. The number one problem is *greed*. Have you ever known someone who just could not be content no matter how much they had? I was once like this myself. Of course, I didn't think of it at the time as being greedy. I just always wanted more than I had.

Hebrews 13:5 says, "Let your character or moral disposition be free from love of money [including greed, avarice, lust, and craving for earthly possessions] and be satisfied with your present [circumstances and with what you have]; for He [God] Himself has said, I will not in any way fail you nor give you up nor leave you without support. [I will] not, [I will] not, [I will] not in any degree leave you helpless nor forsake nor let [you] down (relax My hold on you)! [Assuredly not!]" Wow! That is powerful!

This Scripture lets us know that we can and should be satisfied where we are, while we are getting to where we are going. God's ways are progressive. He has a wonderful plan for our lives and it unfolds progressively. We don't have to wait until we have the end result to enjoy where we are and be satisfied. We can find our satisfaction in Him while we are on our way to the fulfillment of our hopes and dreams.

I also believe that *fear* causes many of us to be unhappy and discontented. We are afraid we will not get what we desire. At one time, I had a misconceived notion that I had to pray my fearful feelings away and continue praying for God to deliver me until those feelings were all gone. I have since learned that I don't have to submit to those fearful feelings. I learned that I could do the things God wanted me to do, and I could wait on His perfect timing to bring to me those things that He knew were best for me. If I hadn't learned that lesson, I wouldn't be teaching and preaching today.

We can find our satisfaction in Him while we are on our way to the fulfillment of our hopes and dreams.

Once we learn to trust God and step

out even though we're afraid, God will provide the courage and boldness we need to overcome our fear. Just remember that there are no
failures in Christ. If you make a mistake, God will just lift you up,
teach you something from it, and send you on your way. You have
not failed until you stop trying.

Lack of trust in God is another cause of discontentment. Simple
trust in God brings us into a place of rest. Romans 15:13 says, "May
the God of your hope so fill you with all joy and peace in believing
[through the experience of your faith] that by the power of the Holy
Spirit you may abound and be overflowing (bubbling over) with
hope." Joy and peace are found in believing. Simple, childlike faith
brings us the kingdom, which is righteousness, peace, and joy.

Looking for contentment in all the wrong places is my fourth reason
for discontentment. For years I looked for contentment and satisfaction in things. The result was that I never found it. I was never really
satisfied. My husband, Dave, told me once that he had finally realized that no matter what he did, he could never satisfy me, so he was
going to quit working so hard at it.

The prophet Jeremiah refers to looking for satisfaction in all
the wrong places as digging empty wells that have no water in
them (see Jeremiah 2:13 NCV). The answer to my constant frustration came when I received the revelation that my satisfaction had to
be in Christ Jesus. I came to know what a privilege it was to live
under His guidance, trusting that He would never fail me, nor forsake me.

When Paul said he had learned to be content, he was saying that
even if he did not particularly like the situation in which he found
himself, he still trusted God. Therefore, his trust kept him in perfect
peace. When our mind is stayed on the Lord, we are content and
peaceful.

Trusting God and refusing to complain in hard times greatly hon-
ors Him. It is of no value to talk of how much we trust God when all
is well. But when the test comes, then we should say and sincerely
mean, "I trust You, Lord." He delights in a contented child. When we

stop struggling with everything and humble ourselves under the mighty hand of God, He promises to exalt us.

God is waiting to bless you, but you must close destructive doors of discontentment through gratitude and thanksgiving. He always knows what He is doing. Don't wait until everything is perfect before you decide to enjoy your everyday life.

2

Have You Been Struggling
with Yourself?

These are challenging times for everyone, but particularly, for Christian women. We struggle over whether or not to work outside the home, while being constantly aware of the need for additional finances. We are troubled by the ever-present dangers our children face in just attending school at whatever level, from preschool to college. Such dangers were not even issues when we were growing up.

We feel guilty when we're unable to accept a leadership position in the church because of time constraints, family issues, and simply feeling inadequate about our qualifications. Let's face it, from time to time, we find ourselves just wanting to give up.

Growing up spiritually is not easy, but now is not the time to give up or give in. I am reminded of Galatians 6:9, which says, "Let us not lose heart and grow weary and faint in acting nobly and doing right, for in due time and at the appointed season we shall reap, if we do not loosen and relax our courage and faint."

That is an encouraging word for you and me today. Perhaps you have been struggling with yourself. You want to change. You desire to be more like Jesus. And yet you feel as though you're making no progress in your Christian walk at all. Something I want you to realize is that *you are making progress*. Little by little, from glory to glory, day after day, you are changing.

I have lived with my husband for many, many years. He looks the same to me as he did the day I married him . . . until I look at our wedding pictures. Then I see that he has changed. Little changes have occurred each day—but because I am with Dave all the time, I haven't even noticed them. The same is true with each of us. We are with ourselves all the time, and because of this, we don't realize how much we are changing.

Take a minute to think about where you were when you first accepted Jesus into your heart. You will find that you have changed more than you think. We all need to realize that we're on a journey, and we are making progress. It is only the lies of Satan that can defeat us with feelings of failure. He continually seeks to remind us about how far we have to go. He is certainly never going to comfort us concerning how far we've come. Allow the Holy Spirit to encourage you.

The way to listen to the Holy Spirit is by following your heart—not your head or your feelings. We women are often moved by feelings, but we can't trust them. We have to learn to live beyond feelings—to dig down into the deeper places within us where the spirit of God dwells. The devil may say to your head, "You are a failure. You will never change." But if you get quiet and ask God what He has to say about you, you'll hear something like, "You are My child, and I love you. I am changing you and doing a work in your life. Don't listen to the lies of the enemy. Keep your eyes on Me, for I will uphold you and cause you to stand."

Try meditating on those words when the enemy attacks you with feelings of doubt and tempts you to give up on yourself and God. You will begin to see a major difference. *Why believe a liar?* Satan is the father of lies, and the truth is not in him (see John 8:44). We must cast down every imagination that does not agree with the Word of God (see 2 Corinthians 10:5).

We have to learn to live beyond feelings—to dig down into the deeper places within us where the spirit of God dwells. ☺

Be patient with yourself. Keep pressing on and believing that you are changing every day because of the Spirit of God that is working in your life. Be a good student of God's Word. It is the truth that will set you free. Don't compare yourself with other women.

Even women who look as though they've never made a mistake in their entire lives have made mistakes. We all have strengths and weaknesses.

Allow the Holy Spirit to correct you and don't feel rejected when He does. Father God corrects us out of His love for us, because He desires that we become all we can be. He wants us to be transformed into the image of Himself. Don't give up! You're growing up. You're maturing in Christ. There are some growing pains in the process, but each one you feel means that you are a little closer to the finish line.

Paul said in Acts 20:24, "But none of these things move me; neither do I esteem my life dear to myself, if only I may finish my course with joy." Be willing to die to self. Let Christ be your real life. Grow up into Him Who is the Head, and you will ultimately be a woman who knows joy unspeakable and full of glory!

Pray About Everything and Worry About Nothing!

*T*he Bible has much to say about how we are to handle worry, anxiety, care, and concern. First Peter 5:7 always comes to my mind initially, because my husband is such a champion "care caster." It says, "Casting the whole of your care [*all* your anxieties, *all* your worries, *all* your concerns, once and for all] on Him, for He cares for you affectionately and cares about you watchfully." That's good news—news that Dave got down on the inside of him way before I did.

I was a worrier, but I learned that worry, anxiety, and care literally have no positive effect on our lives. They never bring a solution to problems, and they prevent our growth in the Word of God. Look with me at Mark 4:19, "Then the cares and anxieties of the world and distractions of the age, and the pleasure and delight and false glamour and deceitfulness of riches, and the craving and passionate desire for other things creep in and choke and suffocate the Word, and it becomes fruitless."

I believe that one of Satan's number one ways to steal the Word from the heart of a committed Christian woman is through cares. As women, we need our hearts to be free to meditate on God's Word. Our families need us to be women of the Word so that we can receive revelation for how we are to live, both individually and as a family unit.

> *When our minds are constantly on ourselves, our problems, and our personal needs, we become ineffective and powerless.* ◡

Our employers need us to be women of the Word so they can trust and depend on our God-given wisdom and understanding. Our churches need us to be women of the Word so we can help meet the needs of others there and in our communities.

This only comes when God's truths are rooted in our hearts. When our minds are constantly on ourselves, our problems, and our personal needs, we become ineffective and powerless. Philippians 4:6 reminds us not to "fret or have any anxiety about anything, but in every circumstance and in everything, by prayer and petition (definite requests), with thanksgiving, continue to make your wants known to God." This instruction is clear: Do not take care upon yourself.

We need to pray about everything and worry about nothing! We need the Lord. When we worry, it shows that we think we can solve our own problems. We are not built to handle problems. We are created by God to be dependent upon Him, to bring Him our challenges in life, and to allow Him to help us with them.

Can you imagine your life without worry? Why not start today to live a worry-free and carefree life? Ask the Lord to show you every time you are taking on care instead of casting it off. When He makes you aware of it, be willing to immediately cast it on Him. You will enjoy life so much more, and your breakthroughs will come faster. After a period of time, you will find it difficult to worry. It will seem like something that just does not suit you any longer.

God has not fashioned women for worry, care, and concern, so cast them off instead of putting them on. The devil will keep offering them to you, but you don't have to accept them. Remember that Jesus wants you to cast all your care on Him because He cares for you! No one—absolutely no one—ever cared for you as much as Jesus. Why not start to enjoy being cared for by the Prince of Peace, the Author and Finisher of your faith, the One who does all things well. You will fall in love with Jesus all over again and peace will settle in over your life.

God has not fashioned women for worry, care, and concern. ☺

4

You Are a Work in Progress

During my years in ministry to others, I have discovered that many women really don't like themselves, which is a much bigger problem than you might initially think. How we feel about ourselves is a determining factor in our success in life and in relationships.

So how do you see yourself?

Our self-image is the inner picture we carry of ourselves. If what we see is not healthy and accurate according to the Bible, we will suffer from fear, insecurity, and various types of misconceptions about ourselves.

Women who are insecure about themselves suffer in their minds and emotions, as well as in their social and spiritual lives. I know this is true because I have talked with thousands of them, and I myself have suffered in this area.

But God never intended for us to feel bad about ourselves. Nobody knows us as well as God. Yet, even though He knows us—and everything about us, including all of our faults—He still approves of us and accepts us. "Before I formed you in the womb I knew and approved of you [as My chosen instrument] . . ." (Jeremiah 1:5). He does not approve of our wrong behavior, but He is committed to us as individuals.

No one is perfect, and you must understand this as you consider how you see yourself. Can you honestly evaluate yourself and your behavior without feeling condemnation? Can you see how far you have come as well as how far you still have to go? In 2 Corinthians 3:18, Paul states that God changes us "from one degree of glory to another."

If you are a born-again woman, then you are somewhere on the path of the righteous. You may not be as far along as you would like to be, but thank God you are on the path. Remember, there was a time when you were totally outside of the covenant relationship with God through unbelief (see Ephesians 2:11,12). But now you belong to the household of God, and you are being transformed by Him day by day. Enjoy the glory you are in right now, and don't worry about others being further along than you. They had to pass through the same place where you are now.

God wants you to realize that you are a unique woman, and that He has a unique plan for you. He wants you to recognize that you are a work in progress and that you should learn to enjoy where you are instead of comparing yourself to others.

When we don't enjoy the glory we are in right now, we slow down the maturing process. I don't believe we can pass into the next degree of glory until we have learned how to enjoy the one we are in at the moment. In this sense, a "glory" is simply a place that is better than the previous one.

I had so many flaws in my personality and character that even after five years of trying to walk with the Lord, I still felt that I had made practically no progress. Yet, all that time I was gradually becoming a little more glorious.

As women, we are usually too hard on ourselves, but we would grow faster if we relaxed more and learned to live by God's Word and not by how we feel. His Word states that as long as we believe, He is working in us.

First Thessalonians 2:13 says, "The Word of God . . . is effectually at work in you who believe [exercising its superhuman power in those who adhere to and trust in and rely on it]." This means we are a work in progress.

I encourage you to say every day, "God is working in me right now—He is changing me!" We must speak what

> *When we don't enjoy the glory we are in right now, we slow down the maturing process.* ☺

the Word says, not what we feel. Too often women talk about how they feel, and when they do that, it is difficult for the Word of God to work in them effectively.

We also must be careful that we don't develop the attitude that if we don't perform perfectly, we will be rejected. The world often operates on that principle, but God doesn't, and neither should we.

We become so accustomed to people in the world being overly concerned about our performance and what we are doing, that we bring wrong thinking into our relationship with God. We mistakenly entertain the possibility that God may feel the same way about us as do the women in the world, and He does not. This fear of being rejected (or not being accepted) is a major hindrance to our succeeding in life and in our spiritual walk with the Lord.

As we step out to be all we can be in Christ, we will make some mistakes—everyone does. But it takes the pressure off us when we realize that God only expects us to do the best we can. He does not expect us to be perfect, totally without flaws. If we were as perfect as we try to be, we wouldn't need a Savior. I believe that God will always leave some defects in us, just so we will recognize how much we need Jesus every single day. But when we learn to see how far we have come, we will know that God is still working on us—that we are a work in progress.

So if you're not as far along in becoming the godly woman you want to be, don't despair. God isn't through with you yet—there are yet many more levels of glory, and I urge you to enjoy every one of them!

5

Frazzled, Frantic, and Frustrated? Do Something About It!

As a busy woman, I'm sure you know about the frustration that comes from all the demands on your time. Sometimes it seems that life gets unorganized and out of control in spite of our best efforts to properly prioritize our activities and manage our time.

I find that sometimes I don't like the way my days are going, but I have learned that I'm the only one who can change it! Too often we murmur and complain while we change nothing. We sometimes pray and ask God to remove the frustration while we do nothing to change the root cause of the problem.

As responsible women, we are supposed to manage our lives, but it seems that too often we allow our lives to manage us. If you feel that your life is managing you, perhaps it's time to take an inventory of what you are doing with your time, money, and talents. Are you living a balanced life . . . getting enough rest, eating properly, spending enough time with God, your family, and having enough solitude for yourself? If you're not happy with the results of such an inventory, I encourage you to ask God to help you make the necessary changes that will help you set your life in order.

The Lord is ready and willing to instruct and lead all of us in a good path that will produce much fruit for us and for the kingdom of God, but we must be willing to follow. So often women live such fragmented lives, they never really accomplish much. What a tragedy, when there is so much potential available.

I find that staying focused is a challenge in today's society. There are many urgent demands that scream at women every day. Why are women having so much trouble with stress? Can it be because they are trying to do too much . . . and are frustrated because they are spending their time doing things that leave them feeling unfulfilled? Much confusion exists in our lives, and yet the Bible clearly says that God is not the author of confusion (see 1 Corinthians 14:33).

The "hurry up" spirit that is so prevalent today adds to the pressure. And, sad to say, many women confess that they feel so extremely busy that their days go by in a blur. Yet they feel that they accomplish very little. I think a surprising number of women would say they sense that their lives are out of control—perhaps even on a crash course—but they don't know what to do about it. They don't like it, but they don't change anything.

Consider the life of Jesus, who is our great example. He was a hard worker and He was busy, yet He always had time for people. He never seemed to be in a hurry, and He was the picture of perfect peace. Jesus knew the secret that many of us miss. He knew how to say yes to Father God and no to people if their requests conflicted. He knew what His mission was, and He used His time and abilities to accomplish His God-given purpose. He was led by the Spirit and was obedient.

Most women will admit that they don't spend as much time with God as they should, and the excuse is almost always "I'm just too busy." We spend time doing "urgent" things and ignore "important" things. We must remember that we cannot single-handedly do everything that needs to be done. We cannot meet every need. We can only successfully do our part. I urge you to make sure that you're spending your time doing what is really important to God—not what is important to everyone else you know. We should always be open to changing our plan to help meet a need if that is the way the Holy Spirit is leading. But don't fall into the trap of feeling obligated. The tyranny of the "shoulds" and "oughts" keep many believers out of God's perfect will for their lives.

Don't fall into the trap of feeling obligated. ☙

It is time to get rid of the things in your life that are not God's priorities for you. Even if you have to make some radical changes, do whatever it takes to align yourself with the perfect will of God.

Remember—if you are frazzled, frantic, and frustrated because your life is out of control, it's time to make some changes. When you "learn to sense what is vital, and approve and prize what is excellent and of real value [recognizing the highest and the best ...]" (Philippians 1:10), you will discover that your life is taking on new meaning and order.

6

Are You Always on Your Mind?

As busy women who sometimes carry overwhelming responsibilities, it is easy for our own needs to be put on hold. This is a common problem today, but it is not God's will for us. The real problem is that after a while, we get tired and burned out, and that's when the devil begins planting thoughts like, "Well, what about me? Does anyone care about my needs?" And unless you know how to strike a balance between the two needs, you can quickly fall into the trap of thinking about "poor me" all the time. And that's not a good place to be.

Having yourself on your mind all the time can make your life miserable. Jesus said in Mark 8:34, "If anyone intends to come after Me, let him deny himself [forget, ignore, disown, and lose sight of himself and his own interests] and take up his cross, and . . . follow with Me."

I can tell you from experience that this is not easy to do. I find that it's a challenge to keep myself off my mind, but the more I obey the Lord's command in this area, the happier I become. I think as women, we generally form the habit of trying to take care of ourselves and make sure that we are well provided for, which is fine as long as we don't leave God out of the process.

True joy only comes from giving your life away—not from striving to keep it.

First Peter 4:19 says that even those who are being ill-treated should "commit their souls [in charge as a deposit] to the One Who created [them] and will never fail [them]." Imagine yourself going by the "drive-through " at the bank and making a deposit of cash. In the same way, we should, by faith, deposit ourselves in God's care.

Obviously, we cannot live without giving some thought to ourselves and making plans, but when we move into a selfish, self-centered mind-set, we are out of balance and out of God's will.

Our society promotes "me-ism," but the Word of God does not. In 2 Timothy 3:1-4, we are instructed to "understand this, that in the last days will come (set in) perilous times of great stress and trouble [hard to deal with and hard to bear]. For people will be lovers of self and [utterly] self-centered . . . proud and arrogant and contemptuous boasters. They will be abusive (blasphemous, scoffing), disobedient to parents, ungrateful, unholy and profane. [They will be] . . . slanderers (false accusers, troublemakers) . . . haters of good . . . inflated with self-conceit. [They will be] lovers of sensual pleasures and vain amusements more than and rather than lovers of God."

It is easy to see that we are living in such a time right now—rubbing shoulders every day with people who exhibit these characteristics. But God forbid that we as Christian women should fall into such deceptive behavior. As God's children, it is imperative that we resist the magnetic pull of these worldly ways and refuse to be excessive in self-centered thinking.

We must be delivered from being the center of our lives, and when we allow the Holy Spirit to help us, He will do that by transforming us into the image of Jesus Christ. Jesus gave His very life for others, so the least we can do is to give of ourselves for the benefit of others. In fact, true joy only comes from giving your life away—not from striving to keep it. Romans 15:2 says, "Let each of us make it a practice to please (make happy) his neighbor for his good and for his true welfare, to edify him [to strengthen him and build him up spiritually]." As you give of yourself to others, instead of only thinking of yourself, God will give back to you and make sure that you are an abundantly blessed woman.

7

Please Don't Make Me Wait!

*W*aiting! It's a big part of our everyday lives, and most of us don't particularly enjoy it . . . or have time for it. Especially, busy women who usually have way more to do in a day than they can possibly accomplish.

But I can tell you from experience that our attitude about waiting can make all the difference in the world. Like the Israelites who spent forty years making an eleven-day trip, I was stuck in a modern-day wilderness of my own. And my attitudes kept me in that wilderness far too long.

Jesus died so we could live in the Promised Land—that land of abundance in every area of our lives. He wants us to have and enjoy "righteousness, and peace, and joy in the Holy Ghost" (Romans 14:17 KJV). Third John 2 says, "Beloved, I pray that you may prosper in every way and [that your body] may keep well, even as [I know] your soul keeps well and prospers." This Scripture makes it very clear that God wants us to be blessed and live in the land of good things.

I was living in bondage in my personal Egypt-world, but God sent me a deliverer. Through the power and leadership of the Holy Spirit, Jesus brought me out and started me on a journey through the wilderness toward the Promised Land. But like the Israelites and many others who are trapped in the wilderness, I kept going round and round the same mountains.

Having a good attitude in a trying situation is at least 90 percent of the battle.

The Israelites felt that their lack of progress was due to having too many enemies, and I felt the same way. I was sure that if I had enjoyed a better start in life—if I hadn't been abused and mistreated—things would be different.

I was sure that if I'd had more money, felt better physically, or had achieved more success, I would be making faster progress. There was always some "reason" why I was not progressing, but it was never "me."

The Israelites wandered around in the wilderness for forty years murmuring, grumbling, complaining, and blaming Moses and God for their troubles. They just generally felt sorry for themselves. They thought their lack of progress was due to their enemies—but, in fact, it was their attitudes.

Having a good attitude in a trying situation is at least 90 percent of the battle. We can win over anything as long as we have a godly attitude. There will always be trials in life, but as we trust God and continue to do what He is showing us to do, we will always come out victorious.

I had many wrong attitudes that contributed to the prevention of my progress, but the major roadblock for me was an impatient attitude that made me want to scream: *Please don't make me wait for anything. I deserve everything immediately!*

I had a long and interesting journey before I learned that waiting is part of our walk with God. We *will* wait—that is a given—but it is *how* we wait that determines how difficult and long the wait will be.

When you arrive for an appointment with your doctor or dentist, you have to wait your turn. The first thing the receptionist tells you is "Please have a seat while you're waiting." Being seated indicates that a person is resting, and that's exactly what we should do, both in the doctor's office and in the wilderness experiences of our lives. While we're waiting for God to deliver us from our enemies, we should rest in Him.

While we're waiting for God to deliver us from our enemies, we should rest in Him. ☺

Hebrews 4:3 teaches that those who have believed enter into the rest of God. Works of the flesh make us miserable and wear us out, but those who enter the rest of God are able to enjoy the journey. You can also learn to enjoy the wait!

Another wilderness attitude that prevented me from making progress was "I will do it my way or not at all." The stubborn attitude is one that many people have to deal with. If it is not dealt a death-blow, promised-land living becomes a shadow and never a reality—something we see off in the future but never experience.

But it doesn't have to be that way. When we are serious about making some changes and will allow the Holy Spirit to help us, we can take a shortcut through the wilderness instead of going the long way around!

Don't be afraid of God's searchlight—that's how He exposes our faults so we can work together to remove them. It is an uncomfortable process, but the discomfort is temporary. Not facing the truth can leave us with permanent discomfort. So pray for truth, cooperate with God in the attitude adjustments, and then rest in the knowledge that He loves you very much. When He has accomplished His work in your life, you will be a real woman of faith who can walk out of the wilderness into the abundant life He had planned for you all along.

8

Back to the Devil!

l is alive and well today, and that he is always
assault. First Peter 5:8 tells us to "be vigilant
...es; for that enemy of yours, the devil, roams
around like a lion roaring [in fierce hunger], seeking someone to
seize upon and devour."

As wise women, we must constantly be on guard against his
attacks. In order to know how to defend ourselves against the devil
and his evil plans for us, it is important that we know and understand some of his characteristics.

You will notice that Peter did not say the devil *is* a lion. It says he is
like a lion. He is merely a pretender and a phony. And he's also a liar.
John 8:44 tells us that there is no truth in him. The devil doesn't like
Christians, and he uses his deceptive lies to try to lead us astray. And
unfortunately, sometimes he succeeds. When people are deceived
through his lies and deception, it is difficult for them to obtain freedom because they don't realize they have been deceived. But there is
a way to freedom.

Jesus died that we might be free, and freedom comes from knowing the truth. He said, "If you abide in My word [hold fast to My
teachings and live in accordance with them] . . . you will know the
Truth, and the Truth will set you free" (John 8:31). It is easy to see
that God operates through truth and light and that Satan works
through darkness and deception. One of the best ways to defend ourselves against the devil is to know the Word of God and to speak it
aloud against the lies he sends to bombard our minds.

Second Corinthians 10:4,5 teaches us that "the weapons of our warfare are not physical [weapons of flesh and blood], but they are mighty before God for the overthrow and destruction of strongholds, [inasmuch as we] refute arguments and theories and reasoning and every proud and lofty thing that sets itself up against the [true] knowledge of God; and we lead every thought and purpose away captive in to the obedience of Christ (the Messiah, the Anointed One)."

The devil often attacks us by bringing wrong thoughts to our minds, but these strongholds are destroyed when we bring our thoughts into captivity to the knowledge of the Word of God that we have inside of us. The light of His Word exposes the devil's deceptions, and then we must continually resist allowing the enemy to control our minds with those thoughts. We do that by using the weapon of the Word and talking back to the devil.

We can show the devil that we're not wimpy women who will fall for his tricks. We can let him know that we will not stand idly by and let him fill our heads full of junk that doesn't line up with God's Word. We can follow the example Jesus set when the devil tempted Him in the wilderness. He talked back to the devil, answering each of his attacks with the phrase "It is written," and quoting the truths of God's Word.

When the devil tells you that you are no good, that you will never amount to anything, and that God doesn't love you, do warfare using the Word of God. Get out your two-edged sword and use it! Talk to the devil loud and clear, saying, "I am the righteousness of God in Jesus Christ" (2 Corinthians 5:21). "God has a good plan for my life" (Jeremiah 29:11), and "nothing can separate me from the love of God" (Romans 8:35-39).

> *When the devil tells you that you are no good, that you will never amount to anything, and that God doesn't love you, do warfare using the Word of God.* ∽

When we know the character of God, it is easy to trust Him and confidently declare the truths of His Word. The Bible tells us that He is faithful, merciful, just, kind, good, and loving. But the Word also teaches us about the character of Satan and how to recognize when he is working so we can defeat him. Everything about the devil brings us down—he depresses, discourages, disappoints, deceives, disillusions, kills, steals, and brings despair and destruction.

I believe there are many women who just stand by and allow the devil to tear up their lives because of a lack of knowledge. That is the place I was in many years ago. The devil was using his lies and evil schemes to keep my life torn up, and I didn't even know he was my real enemy. But I discovered that he is alive and well on planet Earth, that he hated me (and all of God's children), and that he was trying to destroy me. But, thank God, I also learned that through Christ I have authority over the devil, and when I began exercising that authority over him, he no longer had power over my life.

If you have been allowing the devil to tear you up, I encourage you to stand up to him instead of allowing him to rule your life. Luke 10:19 tells us that we have been given authority over the power that the enemy possesses. So start using your God-given power and authority today. Stand up to him and talk back. Follow Jesus' example, by reminding the devil that he is a defeated foe by quoting the Word of God to him. James 4:7 says, "Resist the devil [stand firm against him], and he will flee from you." When the devil sees that you are a woman who knows how to use the weapons of warfare, he won't hang around—he'll be on the run!

9

Choose Faith Instead of Fear

ℋave you ever run away from something, disobeyed God, or started something and then backed down because of a fear? It seems to be a common problem. Many women today struggle with fear and insecurity.

Fear is a tactic the devil uses to hinder your faith and keep you from accomplishing God's will for your life, but you don't have to fall prey to his evil devices. The first step to overcoming fear is to recognize where it comes from.

The Bible tells us that "God did not give us a spirit of timidity (of cowardice, of craven and cringing and fawning fear), but [He has given us a spirit] of power and of love and of calm and well-balanced mind and discipline and self-control" (2 Timothy 1:7).

There are hundreds of references in the Bible that tell people to "fear not." Every person in the Bible who was ever used by God to any degree was told over and over by Him to "fear not."

Fear is nothing more than a feeling that causes certain manifestations. It may cause us to tremble, turn red, sweat, or have shaky knees. But the Bible doesn't say, "Sweat not," "Tremble not," or "Shake not"—it says, "Fear not!"

The Greek word for *fear* implies "flight" or "running away from something." When the Bible says, "Fear not," it doesn't mean, "Don't *feel* fear." God is

When the devil tries to put fear on you, remind him—and yourself—that you are anointed and that God has promised to lead and guide you. ⌒

saying, "When fear comes, don't run away—don't let it stop you from going forward!"

Even though I am a very bold person now, there was a time when I wasn't walking in the confidence and blessings God had for me. My early years were rooted in fear. The spirit of fear was my constant companion. A variety of fears invaded my thoughts on a regular basis, including: fear of harm, fear of rejection, fear of man, fear of the future, fear of people knowing I was being abused, fear of never being loved, fear that my life was ruined, and many others. But through the years, God has helped me understand how the bondages of fear took hold in my life, and He has shown me how to get free.

As a woman of God, you also can be free by choosing to use the "spirit of power" that God has given to you. When the devil tries to put fear on you, remind him—and yourself—that you are anointed and that God has promised to lead and guide you. If you're in a new place, boldly confront the future. The great *I AM* lives in you, so don't be afraid.

I heard a powerful true story about how one woman dealt with fear. She wasn't free to do what she really wanted because fear stopped her when she started to step out. Then one day, a friend spoke three simple but profound words to her that set her free: "Do it afraid."

Whoever said women of faith can't do it afraid? Fear causes us to have adverse feelings, but just because we *feel* fear doesn't mean we can't do the thing we're afraid to do. We have a choice.

I encourage you to make the right choice. Don't let fear keep you from moving forward into God's good plan for your life. Choose to exhibit faith and boldness and start enjoying the wonderful liberating freedom from fear. You'll be glad you did!

10

Don't Leave God out of the Loop

$\mathcal{I}$ believe that women who have learned to be self-sufficient and to take their responsibilities seriously sometimes have difficulty determining where to draw the line. These are very admirable attributes, but when they get out of balance, they can actually hinder your spiritual growth.

As Christian women, we know that we are saved by grace through faith because Ephesians 2:8,9 says, "It is by free grace (God's unmerited favor) that you are saved (delivered from judgment and made partakers of Christ's salvation) through [your] faith. And this [salvation] is not of yourselves [of your own doing, it came not through your own striving], but it is the gift of God . . . [It is not the result of what anyone can possibly do, so no one can pride himself in it or take glory to himself.]"

We know and understand that salvation is a gift of God's grace—that it cannot possibly be earned—and we accept that. But grace is also the power of God to help us in other areas in which we cannot help ourselves. In John 15:5, Jesus tells us, "Apart from Me . . . you can do nothing." This makes it pretty clear that we need help in every area of our lives. If we are to live victoriously, we must realize our impotence and exercise faith in God's grace. He is more than willing to help us if we are willing to give up our independent attitudes.

In Galatians 2:21, the apostle Paul said that if he did not receive the grace, he would be treating His gift as something of minor importance, defeating its purpose and nullifying its effect. God's grace is always flowing to us in every situation, but it must be received by faith. In verse 20, Paul said that it was no longer he who lived, but Christ Who lived in him, and that the life he was now living, he was living by faith in the Son of God.

I discovered years ago that every time I became frustrated it was because I was trying to do something myself, in my own strength, instead of putting my faith in God and receiving His grace, His help. I was frustrated and struggling with something most of the time during the early years of my walk with the Lord. So receiving a revelation of God's grace was a major breakthrough for me. I was always "trying" to do something and leaving God out of the loop. I tried to change myself, and I tried to change my husband and children. I tried to get healed, to prosper, and to make my ministry grow. I tried to change every circumstance in my life that I didn't like. But I only became more frustrated because none of my trying was producing any good results.

God will not permit us to succeed without Him. If He did, we would take the credit that is due Him. If we could change people, we would be changing them to suit our purposes, which would steal their freedom to make their own choices.

I finally learned to pray for what I thought needed to be changed and then turned it over to God to do it His way in His timing. Once I understood grace, it was a matter of learning to trust Him more completely.

I had to practice trusting God for a lot of things, but particularly finances. At one point in the beginning of my ministry, God asked me to trust Him to provide for my family financially without my working outside the home. I knew that I needed time to prepare for the ministry He had called me to. And working full-time in addition to being a wife and mother to three small children didn't leave much time to prepare to be an international Bible teacher.

As an act of faith and with my husband's consent, I quit my job and began learning to trust God to provide for us. Dave had a good job, but his salary was forty dollars a month less than our bills. This meant we had to have a miracle from God every month just to meet our regular expenses.

I remember what a struggle it was not to go back to work—after all, I was a responsible woman and wanted to do my part. But I knew that I had to trust God. Each month He provided for our financial needs, and seeing His faithfulness was exciting, but I was accustomed to taking care of myself—all this "walking by faith" was crucifying my flesh big time. It was difficult for me to keep practicing trust, but eventually I learned to walk by faith in this area. Gaining that strong foundation of faith in the beginning of our ministry has served us well in trying times through the years.

I also had to practice trusting God concerning submission to authority. I had been hurt and mistreated by authority figures in my life, especially male figures, and those experiences had left me quite determined to do things my own way and not trust other people. Of course, the Word of God says that wives should submit to their husbands (Ephesians 5:22 KJV), and I found this to be very difficult. Like most married couples, Dave and I have very different personalities, and I didn't agree with many of his opinions and decisions. However, none of this changed God's Word, so I had to learn to submit whether I wanted to or not. Once again, practicing faith in this area crucified my flesh.

I vividly recall saying to the Lord in a particularly difficult situation, "How can You ask me to trust people after the things that people have done to me?"

He replied to my heart, "I am not asking you to trust people, Joyce. I'm asking you to trust Me."

We grow in grace by practicing putting our faith in God and receiving His grace in situations that are difficult or impossible for us. ☺

He wanted me to trust Him to bring justice in my life in each situation and to realize that if I did not get my own way, then perhaps I was wrong, or He had a better way or different timing in mind. It wasn't easy, but I practiced over and over in this area, and finally I gained victory.

We only learn to trust God by doing it. We grow in grace by practicing putting our faith in God and receiving His grace in situations that are difficult or impossible for us.

If you are struggling with something in your life, ask yourself honestly if you are putting your faith in God, believing that His grace will meet the need, or if you are relying on your own abilities and leaving Him out of the loop? Grace is God's power coming into your situation to do for you what you cannot do for yourself, but you must choose to trust Him and receive His gift of grace. When you keep God in the loop by trusting Him to help you in the difficult areas of your life, you will become a woman of faith who enjoys the abundant grace of God.

11

Believe in the Favor of God

$\mathcal{G}$ suppose that all of us have given or received a favor, which is defined as "an act of kindness; effort in one's behalf or interest." A favor, whether given or received, is a very pleasant experience. I guess that's why God likes to bestow favor on His children. The psalmist David spoke about the favor of God in Psalm 30:5: "His anger is but for a moment, but His favor is for a lifetime or in His favor is life."

There are many people spoken of in the Bible who received God's favor. And since "God shows no partiality and is no respecter of persons" (Acts 10:34), women today can believe for and receive favor in our daily lives.

God's favor is available to us, but like many other good things in life, just because something is available to us doesn't mean that we will partake of it. The Lord makes many things available to us that we never receive and enjoy because we never activate our faith in that area.

I needed a lot of favor to get to where I am today in ministry. I believe I have succeeded at being the person God intended me to be, but it could never have happened without His favor. For example, when we began our television ministry in 1993, hardly anyone even knew Joyce Meyer existed. I knew we would need a lot of favor from God if we were to get on quality television stations around the world. I knew that God had to open doors for us. I was willing to walk through them boldly, but He had to open them and not only give me favor with television station owners and managers, but also with television audiences.

I am a very bold, straightforward, tell-it-like-it-is woman, and many people don't accept that type of personality very well. So I knew that I needed God's favor in this venture of faith. I needed Him to show people my heart and cause them to believe that I wanted to help them.

I think all women have some personality quirks that can turn some people off, so praying for favor is a wise thing to do. When God gives favor, people favor us—and often for no reason they can even explain. If three people applied for the same position and were all equally qualified, the one living under the favor of God would get it.

Favor is actually a part of grace. In the English New Testament, the word *grace* and the word *favor* are both translated from the same Greek word *charis*. So the grace of God is the favor of God. And the favor of God is the grace of God—that which causes things to happen in our lives that need to happen through the channel of faith—the power of God doing something for us that we can neither earn nor deserve.

When we say to someone, "Can you do me a favor?" we are asking that person to do something for us that we have neither earned nor paid for. We are depending on that individual's goodness to manifest in the form of a blessing, even though there is no natural reason for it to be given.

Esther, Daniel and the Hebrew children, Ruth and even Jesus received favor from God that caused them to be accepted instead of being rejected in specific situations. They may have been rejected in some areas, but they were accepted regarding the things God had sent them to do.

As women of God, we should pray for supernatural favor on a regular basis and expect to receive it. ☺

I don't experience total acceptance and favor everywhere I go, and neither does anyone else. But I have experienced great favor as far as people receiving my teaching ministry. I have been invited to speak in some of the finest conferences in the world today, alongside great men and women of God whom I respect and admire. I know it is a manifestation of the favor of God, and I appreciate it.

Esther needed favor with the king. She was selected by God to bring deliverance to her people, who were in danger. She stepped out in faith and went into a place that was hard for her in the natural. God gave her the favor she was believing for, and she fulfilled His call on her life.

Ruth was a Moabite, so there was no way for her to be accepted by the Israelites without favor from God, because the Moabites were idolaters. But God gave her that favor because she loved and trusted Him. She did nothing special to deserve it, but her heart was right with God. Due to His favor, she married Boaz, "a man of great wealth" (Ruth 2:1 NKJV), and their ancestral line brought forth David from whom Jesus was descended.

I think we can see that favor is very valuable and necessary in order to succeed at being all God intends for us to be. As women of God, we should pray for supernatural favor on a regular basis and expect to receive it. To be very honest, it is just plain fun to watch God favor us in certain situations.

I'm sure that you have had times of receiving favor, and that you enjoyed it very much. But I believe God wants to give you even more, so I encourage you to release your faith in this area in a greater way than ever before. Don't be afraid to ask God to give you favor. Ask for it, believe it, and then receive it with joy.

12

You Can Bless Yourself!

$\mathcal{I}$ have found that most of us don't use our mouths for the purpose for which God gave them to us. There is great power and authority in words—and the kind of power depends on the kind of words we speak. We can bless or curse ourselves with our mouths. Early in my Christian walk, God dealt with me about my attitudes, thoughts, and words. In fact, He probably has dealt with me more consistently about my mouth than about any other issue.

As women, we usually desire a mixture of both spiritual and material things. We want to grow spiritually and be used by God, and we want to be blessed in our material circumstances.

There were times when I desired things that would have come under the category of "blessings." But because I hadn't yet learned the importance of my spoken words, I said that I would probably never see these blessings come to pass. Since I spoke according to my experience, I was cursing my future with my own words! I was agreeing with the devil instead of with God.

I needed to call those things that were not as if they were (see Romans 4:17). I needed to call forth from the spiritual realm what I desired. I needed to cooperate with God's good plan for my life, but I was deceived! I was believing lies. Satan is a deceiver. He strives to give us trouble and then uses it to influence us to prophesy that same kind of trouble in our own future!

God has given us words, and He expects us to be accountable for the power that is carried in them. $\backsim$

The prophet Isaiah said that we can bless ourselves! "So [it shall be] that he who invokes a blessing on himself in the land shall do so by saying, May the God of truth and fidelity . . . bless me; and he who takes an oath in the land shall swear by the God of truth and faithfulness to His promises . . . because the former troubles are forgotten and because they are hidden from My eyes" (Isaiah 65:16).

There is a twofold life principle that can be carried into every area in which we desire victory: (1) Nobody's words have as much authority in our lives as our own. (2) Our future cannot be blessed until we let go of the past.

We can begin to think in agreement with God the moment that we mentally stop living in the past. I always say that words are containers for power. "Death and life are in the power of the tongue, and they who indulge in it shall eat the fruit of it [for death or life]" (Proverbs 18:21). That sounds like power to me. And with power comes responsibility. God has given us words, and He expects us to be accountable for the power that is carried in them.

James 3:2 says, "If anyone does not offend in speech [never says the wrong things], he is a fully developed character and a perfect man, able to control his whole body and to curb his entire nature." Take notice of the things you say when you get up in the morning and throughout your day. Whether or not you think so, it does matter—to you and to your well-being. Speak about your situation what you believe Jesus would say, and you will open the door for the miracle-working power of God.

13

Becoming God's Friend

On Luke 11:5-6, Jesus asks, "Which of you who has a friend will go to him at midnight and will say to him, Friend, lend me three loaves [of bread], for a friend of mine who is on a journey has just come, and I have nothing to put before him." A *friend* is defined in Webster's Dictionary as "a person you know, like, and trust; an acquaintance, an associate, one allied with you in a struggle, a comrade, a supporter, one fighting on your side."

I really believe that most women understand the value of friendship, and when God is your friend, you can go to Him with all of your needs, including those of someone who is also your friend. The best thing to do when someone in need comes to you for help is to realize that you don't have what it takes to meet the need—but you know Someone who does. It all depends on whether or not you are a friend of God. When you take God as your partner in life and you're not interested in doing anything without Him, then you are a true friend of God.

Some women are not getting their needs met because they are insecure about their relationship with God. So if they don't get an immediate answer the first time they pray about something, they just run off somewhere and forget about it.

When you know that you are God's friend—it gives you boldness to approach Him again and again when necessary.

But when you know that you are God's friend—it gives you boldness to approach Him again and again when necessary. This friendship causes you to press in to receive things that you know are yours. Knowing that you are a friend of God causes you to be shamelessly persistent until you feel victory in your spirit. When that happens, you will feel a release that allows you to go ahead and enjoy your life, knowing that God is answering your prayer.

Unfortunately, many women are afraid to expect anything from God. But there is nothing wrong with telling God what you are expecting. Hebrews 4:16 says, "Let us then fearlessly and confidently and boldly draw near to the throne of grace (the throne of God's unmerited favor to us sinners), that we may receive mercy [for our failures] and find grace to help in good time for every need [appropriate help and well-timed help, coming just when we need it]."

We women must learn how to take authority in the spirit realm. Friendship with the Lord involves prayer, and prayer is all about moving in faith and getting situations changed. It is intimate conversation between you and Father God. It is about being on the earth and calling for the power of God to come down from heaven to earth to meet the need we're discussing with Him. Yes, we need to balance bold authority with meekness, humility, and gentleness, but taking bold authority is important to our relationship with God. It is in our prayer lives—those private conversational times alone with Him—that we become His friend.

Don't wait until you're perfect to become God's friend. It will never happen, because we will always need some finishing touches. We just need to get up every day and do the best we can to live out of the Word. That's where we get to really know *about* Him, and then in prayer and personal time with Him, we come to *know* Him. He wants to be the kind of friend we can come to boldly with our love as well as our needs.

14

Women Who Walk the Walk

$\mathcal{I}$ recently saw a friend at the grocery store, and I could tell that she really wanted to stop and chat. However, I had an appointment about thirty minutes from the store, and I had to quickly explain that I couldn't talk right then, but had to run.

Later that evening, I felt a prompting in my heart that my friend may not have understood my seeming disinterest in her at the store. I called and let her know that I was sorry I couldn't visit, explaining that I had to keep that appointment, because I'd already canceled it once before.

Now, years ago I wouldn't have done that. I would have taken the attitude "If she was offended, that is her problem." But I've learned that I want to be a woman of God who walks the walk—not just another person who talks the talk. I genuinely try to walk in love and strive not to offend anyone if I can possibly avoid it.

Because of my own experience, I have come to believe that people who are easily offended are usually selfish and insecure as I once was. But 1 Corinthians 13 teaches us that love is not touchy or easily offended. A woman who has her love tank full is secure. We should be continually receiving the love of God, which allows us to be secure and confident. That same chapter says that love is not selfish. When I walk in love, I am not so caught up in how I feel, but I care more about what is going on in the lives of others than what is going on in mine.

We should be continually receiving the love of God, which allows us to be secure and confident. $\mathcal{I}$

Loving someone always costs something. Loving us cost God and His Son Jesus the ultimate price. And when we walk in love with others, it will cost us something—perhaps some money, some time, or even humbling ourselves to be sure we did not offend anyone.

Obviously, some people will get offended no matter what you do. Trying to prevent that type of individual from being offended leaves you no freedom. There is balance in all things, but this is a biblical principle that cannot be ignored. Paul said that we must adjust and adapt ourselves to others (see 1 Corinthians 10:32-33). This type of behavior is far better than giving offense and perhaps hindering someone's salvation or progress in the Lord.

Pride, of course, will not allow us to adapt and adjust to others. Pride wants to control and be right all the time. Humility allows us to yield. Ecclesiastes 10:4 reminds us, "If the temper of the ruler rises up against you, do not leave your place [or show a resisting spirit]; for gentleness and calmness prevent or put a stop to great offenses."

This doesn't mean that we have to become a doormat for everyone to walk on, but most of the things people have problems with are not worth fighting and arguing about anyway. It is far better to go the extra mile in order to glorify God than to stubbornly insist on having our own way—even at the expense of causing great offense.

I wonder how often we have considered a person to be an "enemy" simply because she spoke some truth that we did not want to hear. She might have become a great friend. I am sure that the spirit of offense is a tremendous thief of good friendships. When we ask a question, many of us really don't want the truth. We want people to tell us what we want to hear. Maturity can face truth. Though painful, maturity understands the phrase "No pain, no gain."

I had lots of bondage in my life as a result of years of abuse and running from the truth. As I entered into a deep relationship with the Holy Spirit, He rapidly began to confront me with truth. It was very painful, and frequently I felt that I couldn't stand to go on, but God gave me grace and helped me continue making progress.

How about you? I think I can safely say that with each step of progress we make on our journey with the Lord, we are confronted by a new truth about ourselves. Something old has to pass away before the new can come. You may have an old mind-set, old ways of talking or acting—and God will confront you with the truth about where you are so you can leave that place and step up to the next level. Why? Because He loves you that much!

Matthew 24:10 tells us that "many will be offended" in these last days. Let us agree together that we won't be among them! Guard against offense. It poisons lives and attitudes and steals your love walk. "Keep and guard your heart with all vigilance and above all that you guard, for out of it flow the springs of life" (Proverbs 4:23). Walk in love. Become known as a woman of God who walks the walk that Jesus has laid out for each and every one of us.

15

Determining Your Priorities

The best way I have found to determine if God is first in my life is to slow down and ask myself some simple questions: *What do I think about the most? What is the first thing on my mind in the morning and the last thing on my mind at night? What do I pray and talk about the most? What subjects fill my conversations with God and with others? What do I do with my time?*

If we spend an hour a week praying and five or ten hours a week shopping, then shopping is a higher priority than God. If we spend thirty minutes praying and thirty minutes reading the Bible every week, but spend fifteen hours a week watching soap operas, Oprah, or Dr. Phil on television, then television is a higher priority than God.

The truth is that we make time for what we really want to do. We all have the same amount of hours in a day, and for the most part, we each set our own schedule. If we want to spend time with God, then we are going to make Him a priority.

Let me ask you some questions: What about your money? Is it easy for you to spend money on a new outfit, complete with new jewelry and shoes, or something for your house but difficult to obey God at offering time? Do you find it easier to spend money on eating out than on Christian teaching and music CDs that feed your spirit?

Money in itself is not evil—it's "the love of money [that] is the root of all evil" (1 Timothy 6:10 KJV). If you love God more than money, you can do with your money what God tells you to and be at peace. However, if you love your money more than God, you are probably going to get upset or act like you didn't hear Him when He asks you to do something with it that you don't want to do.

I have nothing against women who want to have enough money to buy things, but I've learned that my trust cannot be in my bank account balance or in the things I've accumulated. And those are things that none of us can afford to trust in. We can lose all of our money and all of our things in an instant. They can be stolen, or the stock market could cave in at any given moment and our money would be worthless. The Bible says, "Do not gather and heap up and store up for yourselves treasures on earth, where moth and rust and worm consume and destroy, and where thieves break through and steal. But gather and heap up and store for yourselves treasures in heaven, where neither moth nor rust nor worm consume and destroy, and where thieves do not break through and steal; for where your treasure is, there will your heart be also" (Matthew 6:19-21).

For us to be truly fulfilled women, you and I need to let God out of the box in which we have placed Him. We need to not limit Him to only an hour or so on Sunday morning. It's true that He is involved in spiritual things like reading the Bible and praying, but He also wants to be a part of our everyday activities like making the beds, doing laundry and vacuuming, going to the grocery store, and even shopping for new clothes, jewelry, and shoes!

Colossians 1:17 says that Jesus "existed before all things, and in Him all things consist (cohere, are held together)." That's the bottom line. The very fact that He is the One Who is holding everything together shows how important He is in relation to everything else. Without Him everything would fall apart.

I challenge you to regularly stop and take a good look at your life. Ask the Holy Spirit to show you where your priorities are out of line. Then allow His conviction to motivate you to seek a deeper relationship with God. Give God all that you are and all that you are not. It is God through the power

Putting God first means to put His ways first—to live the way He would live.

of the Holy Spirit Who will give you the ability to adjust your life-style and bring it in line with the Word (see 1 Thessalonians 5:23). He will enable you to put Him first in your thoughts, conversations, and actions. He will show you how to place Him first in your time, money, relationships, and decision-making.

I am living proof that no matter how big of a mess your life is in, God will turn it around and bless you if you make Him your priority and refuse to quit and give up. Putting God first means to put His ways first—to live the way He would live. John 16:13 reminds us that "the Spirit of Truth . . . will guide you into all the Truth (the whole, full Truth)." Let Jesus be the Lord of your life in everything you do, and you will be more successful and happy than you can imagine.

16

Just Keep It Simple!

For many years, I was a person who did not enjoy life, let alone celebrate it. I was on my way to heaven, but I was not enjoying the trip. But God has taught me a great deal about how to enjoy life. John 10:10 says that Jesus came that we might "have and enjoy life, and have it in abundance (to the full, till it overflows)." What about you? Are you enjoying your life?

I've learned that enjoying life is not based on enjoyable circumstances. It is a heart attitude. Once I discovered that the world was not going to change to accommodate me, I decided to change my approach to some of the circumstances I faced in life. It made a remarkable difference in my life, and I believe with all my heart that it will help you.

Christian women have available to us the abundant quality of life that comes from our God, Who is not full of fear, stress, worry, anxiety, or depression. He is not impatient or in a hurry. He takes time to enjoy His creation. And He wants us to do the same. Unfortunately, I don't really think that the majority of today's women are enjoying their lives. When you dare to ask any of them how they are, their response is nearly always "Busy! I am just so busy with work, the kids, church, school activities, and my husband actually thinks I have time to go to a ball game with him! I can't believe it, Joyce!"

We live in a stressful world that seems to be getting more stressful with each passing year. People are hurrying everywhere. They are rude, short-tempered, and it is easy to see that many women are frustrated and under pressure. They are experiencing financial stress, marital stress, and the stress of raising children in today's world. Their stressful lifestyles cause health problems, which adds more stress.

I have a revelation for you: **Simplicity brings joy and complication blocks it.** Instead of getting entangled with the complications of religion, we must return to the simplicity of believing and maintaining a Father/child relationship. Matthew 18:3 says, "Truly I say to you, unless you repent (change, turn about) and become like little children [trusting, lowly, loving, forgiving], you can never enter the kingdom of heaven [at all]."

Wow! God wants us to approach life with childlike faith. He wants us to grow up in our behavior but remain childlike in our attitude toward Him concerning trust and dependence. He wants us to know that we are His precious little ones—His children. We show faith in Him when we come to Him this way, which releases Him to care for us. I do not believe that we can have peace and enjoy life without childlike faith. When you begin to live your life with all the simplicity of a child, it will change your whole outlook in a most amazing way.

Start looking for ways that you complicate things and ask the Holy Spirit to teach you simplicity. He lives in you, and although He is extraordinarily powerful, He is also extraordinarily simple. He will teach you simplicity if you truly wish to learn.

If you are anything like I was, you may be a workaholic. I found extreme satisfaction in accomplishment, and I often worked when I should have taken the time to do other things—maybe even to spend "fun time" with my family. Take it from me, enjoying life is a gift from God! Our families are also His gift to us. Don't risk having an unbalanced attitude that might lead your family to believe they are less important to you than your busyness and work. Don't allow yourself to get so caught up in that trap that you fail to enjoy the simple pleasures that God provides in every single day.

Simplicity brings joy and complication blocks it. ☺

As women of God, you and I were given life by Him and our goal should be to enjoy it. Let's keep it simple and stop complicating things. Try saying these words when you get up in the morning: "This is the day which the Lord hath made; [I] will rejoice and be glad in it" (Psalm 118:24 KJV).

17

Are You Waiting on God,
or Is God Waiting on You?

*H*ave you ever allowed your emotions and immediate needs to override everything else because you simply could not discipline yourself to wait? How many women do you know who have traded lifetime blessings for short-term appetites?

James 5:7 exhorts us, "So be patient, brethren, [as you wait] till the coming of the Lord. See how the farmer waits expectantly for the precious harvest from the land. [See how] he keeps up his patient [vigil] over it until it receives the early and late rains." This Scripture does not say "be patient *if* you wait." It says to "be patient *as* you wait." Waiting is a part of life. Many women don't "wait well," and yet, we actually spend more time in our lives waiting than we do receiving. I finally decided to learn to enjoy the waiting time, not just the receiving time.

I began to realize that impatience is a fruit of pride, and pride prevents waiting because the proud woman thinks so highly of herself that she believes she should never be inconvenienced in any way. You probably aren't like this, but many women are, and I have to admit that I once was this way. It is dangerous to lift ourselves up to such an elevated place that it causes us to look down on others. A humble woman will not display an impatient attitude.

If you have waited a long time and haven't seen much progress, you are probably getting very tired of waiting. I encourage you to take a fresh attitude toward waiting. God has taught me through His

Word to keep living the life I have now, while I am waiting for things to come to pass that I long for in my heart. We can become so intent on trying to birth the next thing that we do not take care of and enjoy the things at hand.

What kind of woman do you want to be? Are you willing to be stretched, to grow, to mature? Or do you think you have to have what you want now?

The Bible says Jesus endured the cross for the joy of the prize on the other side of that cross (see Hebrews 12:2). Moses chose to suffer hardship and criticism in order to serve God. He was looking beyond what he was going through at the present to the reward and recompense that would come later.

Every one of us must decide. We must pay the price. Jesus never said it would be easy, but He said it would be worth it. Laying down our own will for the will of God is not an easy thing. When the Holy Spirit deals with us, we try to run away, but He won't give up. And He keeps dealing with us until we settle down and let ourselves be guided into the path where He wants us to go.

Willingness is step one. Though He was willing, even Jesus battled through tormenting emotions in the Garden of Gethsemane and made that final decision to do what He was called to do—endure the pain of the cross and become the perfect sacrifice for us all.

I had many sessions with God about my impatience with regard to waiting, but He was faithful to stay with me until I wore myself out and was finally willing to listen to His voice. I am so glad that I went through all those tough encounters with God, because I am now living in the reward. And you can too!

You will go through some things as you learn how to wait patiently. Only God knows what price He's asked you to pay. Nobody has the right to judge or criticize you. Paul answered criticism

As we learn to be obedient while we're in God's waiting room, we grow in our ability and willingness to lay aside our will and do His.

by saying he bore the marks of the Lord Jesus in his body. No one had the right to tell him he was not faithful to God.

Waiting is a test that determines our attitude. When you remain faithful and patient, no one can steal your reward from you. Do whatever it takes to learn not to be so caught up with the immediate need and the thing your flesh is screaming for right now so that you end up losing your long-term blessing. Start today by being willing to wait for God to work out His will for your life.

Victorious living demands prompt, exact obedience to the Lord. As we learn to be obedient while we're in God's waiting room, we grow in our ability and willingness to lay aside our will and do His. It is vital that we make progress in this area.

When your battle with waiting seems endless and you think you won't make it, remember that you are reprogramming a very carnal, fleshly, worldly mind to think as God thinks. Impossible? No! Difficult? Yes! But God is on your side. He is the best "computer programmer" around. Just cooperate with Him and don't give up. Be prepared and ready when God tells you it's time for you to step up and step out in Him. Don't make Him wait on you to respond to His divine call.

18

You Aren't Weird—You're Unique!

*D*o you ever find yourself trying to be like someone you believe is more acceptable than you? Does your heart cry out for freedom to be accepted for who and what you are right where you are? I believe that many, if not most women, feel this way at some point in their lives. But it isn't a very enjoyable way to live. Women who don't accept themselves usually have difficulty getting along with others.

I had a hard time with relationships until I finally realized through the Word of God that my problems in getting along with others were rooted in my difficulties with myself. I did not like my personality. I constantly compared myself with other women, found fault with myself, rejected and even hated myself. I thought I was weird because I was not like everyone else.

God helped me to discover that I'm not weird—I'm unique! And since a unique thing has more value because it's rare, I also have worth! Now I can enjoy the freedom to be myself, and I have discovered that it's one of the greatest gifts God has given me. What I have experienced and enjoyed will work for you too!

You are a rare, one-of-a-kind, valuable, and precious woman. And I want to help you learn how to be successful at being yourself with some easy-to-follow suggestions:

You are a rare, one-of-a-kind, valuable, and precious woman. ☺

1. *Speak good things about yourself.* Declare what God's Word says about you. For example, say to yourself, "I am the righteousness of God in Christ. I am made acceptable in the Beloved. God created me and formed me with

His own hand, and God doesn't make mistakes." (See 2 Corinthians 5:21; Ephesians 1:6; Psalm 119:73). I like to start the day saying good things about myself, the day, the future. Look into the mirror and say aloud, "God loves you, I love you, and I accept you."

2. *Avoid comparing yourself with other women.* God must love variety or all of us wouldn't look so different. He has created each of us differently right down to our fingerprints. We can, of course, look to certain people as good examples to follow—but even then, good traits if duplicated will manifest differently through our individual personalities.

3. *Focus on your potential instead of your limitations.* Refuse to concentrate on your weaknesses except in an effort to turn them into strengths. Keep your flaws in perspective. People with a high level of confidence have just as many weaknesses as those without confidence, but they focus on their strengths—not their weaknesses.

4. *Learn to cope with criticism.* If you dare to be different, you'll have to expect some criticism. Going along with the crowd when you know in your heart that God is leading you in a different direction is one of the reasons women don't succeed at being themselves. You won't be very comfortable in your own skin if you go against your own convictions.

If the devil has tormented you with thoughts about your every fault or paraded other women before you who appear to have no faults, don't believe him. He's just a liar. His lies cause women needless pain and suffering, but the truth of God's Word renews our minds and transforms us into the women God wants us to be. (See Ephesians 4:23-24).

Now is the time to stop pretending to be someone else and start being who you really are. Remember this—God will never anoint you to be anyone other than yourself. Let now be your time to go forward and be set free from the torments of comparisons and trying to be someone you are not. The only thing that stands between you and victory is YOU.

19

Are You Ever Weary?

$\mathcal{D}$o you ever experience weariness? How about "spiritual" burnout? Do you ever feel like giving up—just quitting—because you feel as though you're doing everything you know to do and are getting no right results? Have you ever asked the questions "If God is good, all powerful, and full of love for us, why didn't He stop this? Why did He allow that to happen?" Satan seeks to build a wall between God and hurting women. He is eager to spread the lie that God is not good and cannot be trusted. We know that is not true. We know that God is good—that He cannot be anything else—but trust always requires unanswered questions.

Webster defines the word *weary* as "to be faint, to wear out or be worn out, tired, sick, fatigued, exhausted, and out of patience." We must realize that this is part of Satan's plan for end-time believers. Daniel 7:25 is a vivid description of a vision the prophet Daniel received regarding the last days, "And he . . . shall wear out the saints of the Most High . . . "

Fainthearted is a word used in the Old Testament accounts by Moses, Isaiah, and Jeremiah to describe people who are disheartened and wearied by the events of their times. It means to be "small souled." Your soul is made up of your mind, will, and emotions. This definition says you can't handle challenging problems without caving in, wanting to quit and give up, becoming discouraged, depressed, or negative.

But I want you to be encouraged. There is actually good news! Romans 8:37 confirms that we believers are "more than conquerors and gain a surpassing victory through Him Who loved us"! *More than conquerors* means that before trouble ever starts, we already know who wins. I like that, don't you?

We have purposed in our hearts to maintain such intimate relationship with God and His Word that we are constantly being strengthened by the power of His promises. Intimacy with God produces Christian women who can outlast the devil!

Is it possible that your busy life has crowded out the quality time you once spent with the Lord? Even if you are busy with church or church-related activities, it may be good to compare the time you spend *doing* for God with the time you spend *being* with Him. After all, we are human *beings*—not human *doings*.

I encourage you to learn how to say no when God is telling you not to get involved in this or that activity. You can establish boundaries for your life so you don't get "used up" trying to accomplish something God didn't tell you to do in the first place. Maintaining an intimate relationship with the Lord stores up reserves of His strength from which we can "borrow" as needed.

The word *abide* means "to dwell or live in." It does not refer to visiting. It refers to staying or remaining. I don't visit my house—I live in it. We should learn to live in the love of God. First John 4:16 brings out the point that we should become conscious and aware of the love God has for us. The knowledge of His love should not be some biblical fact to which we mentally assent, but it should be a daily, living reality in our lives. "And we know (understand, recognize, are conscious of, by observation and by experience) and believe (adhere to and put faith in and rely on) the love God cherishes for us. God is love, and he who dwells and continues in love dwells and continues in God, and God dwells and continues in him" (1 John 4:16).

Intimacy with God produces Christian women who can outlast the devil! ☺

You can learn to grow in difficult times as you abide in God's love. Each of us can reap a greater harvest of Christian maturity during difficulties because they force us to press in closer to God. I believe our lives can be lived in such a way that we can really be confident in God's strength—having no fear of the trials and tribulation that produce weary warriors and fainting saints. Spend quality time with the Lord and reap an abundant harvest of His benefits. Remain strong "in Him" and in the power of His might.

20

A Woman of Patience . . .
a Woman of Power

Our world today is in dire need of women who exemplify patience and godly power—women who are "God's own chosen ones (His own picked representatives) . . . who . . . [put] on behavior marked by . . . patience [which is tireless and long-suffering, and has the power to endure whatever comes, with good temper]" (Colossians 3:12).

This Scripture tells us that patience has power. Why is patience powerful? Simply because patient people cannot be controlled by the devil or the circumstances he brings to upset them. The Word of God promises in James 1:4 that a patient person will be "perfectly and fully developed . . . lacking in nothing." Patience is a fruit of the Spirit, and *Vine's Greek Dictionary* states that it grows only under trial.

This is not very exciting news to most of us, but I believe that certain circumstances are set up in our lives to teach us how to deal with unpleasant situations and still remain stable. Jesus went through this, and He tells us that a servant is not above his master (see Matthew 10:24). Jesus remained the same in every situation—He is the Rock, the same yesterday, today, and forever . . . unmovable, unshakable, unsinkable!

Romans 5:3 says, "Moreover, [let us also be full of joy now!] let us exult and triumph in our troubles and rejoice in our sufferings, knowing that pressure and affliction and hardship produce patient and unswerving endurance." We are supposed to be full of joy *now*, not *after* the trial is over. We can only have joy in the midst of trouble if we remember that it is producing something good. Whatever we're going through may not be good, but it can produce something good in us. Patience is a good thing that needs to be developed in us. It cannot flow *through* us, however, unless it has been developed *in* us.

It is vital for the world to see the fruit of the Spirit flowing through believers. Many today read Christians instead of Bibles, and as Christian women, we have many opportunities every day to exhibit patience and power to those in our realm of influence. Certainly we can tell others about the love of God, but it is much more effective if they can see love in action in our lives. The first virtue of love listed in 1 Corinthians 13 is patience: "Love is patient" (see verse 4).

Patience is required to see the fulfillment of God's promises. Hebrews 10:36 says, "You have need of steadfast patience and endurance, so that you may perform and fully accomplish the will of God, and thus receive and carry away [and enjoy to the full] what is promised." We cannot and will not endure without patience. We will not see the end fulfillment of our faith without endurance. Everything does not come to us immediately upon believing. There is waiting involved in receiving from God. It is during these periods of waiting that our faith is tested and purified. Only those who endure and wait patiently will experience the joy of seeing what they have believed for.

It is important to realize that patience is not only an ability to wait, but also how we act while we're waiting. We are encouraged to enter into patient waiting—not just waiting but "patient waiting." It is a given that we will wait. Actually, waiting is a part of life that cannot

> *Patience is required to see the fulfillment of God's promises.* ☙

be avoided. People spend a great deal of time waiting; and if they don't learn to wait patiently, they will be quite miserable. One of the things I have come to realize over the years is that when I am miserable, I usually end up making others miserable also—which, of course, is totally unfair to the people with whom I am in a relationship.

Paul prayed for the church in Colossians 1:11 that they " . . . be invigorated and strengthened with all power according to the might of His glory, [to exercise] every kind of endurance and patience (perseverance and forbearance) with joy."

I believe that as Christian women we can remain calm in the storms of life, control our words, and continue loving others even when their behavior becomes challenging.

It is truly liberating to be free from the control of circumstances through the power of the Holy Spirit and to display the fruit of the Spirit in every situation. God is so patient with us. He is longsuffering, plenteous in mercy, and slow to anger, and we are to imitate Him—to follow Him in every thought, word, and deed. This is impossible without patience. But when you actively pursue the patience of Christ—it will always lead you into His power.

21

De-Stress and Avoid Distress

As a woman dealing with the challenges of living in today's busy world, I'm sure you are familiar with stress. We all deal with a variety of stressors in our lives, but strife causes much of our stress. Nothing is physically harder on me than getting angry or upset—especially if I stay that way for very long. No wonder the Bible says, "When angry, do not sin; do not ever let your wrath (your exasperation, your fury or indignation) last until the sun goes down" (Ephesians 4:26).

In the early years of our marriage, I would get angry and stay that way for days . . . and occasionally for weeks at a time. Being angry and upset seemed to make me more energetic for a while, but when the anger subsided, I felt as if someone had pulled the plug and drained all my energy.

I felt sick much of the time, but I didn't correlate that with my feelings of anger. I had headaches, back trouble, colon trouble, and tension in my neck and shoulders. The doctor ran tests but couldn't find anything wrong with me. He concluded that it was probably stress. That angered me even more! I knew that I was sick, and as far as I was concerned, it wasn't stress that caused it.

I had always been a very intense person—regardless of what I was doing. When I cleaned the house, I worked hard, and I got angry when anyone messed it up. I wanted a house to look at—not to live in. I knew how to work, but I did not know how to live.

This caused strife not only with myself but also with Dave, the children, family members, neighbors, and even God. I did a fair job of hiding it from those I wanted to impress, but my inner life was almost always in turmoil. No matter how well we may hide things from other people, the damage is still going on in our physical bodies and minds if we live under continual stress.

Stress can be mental, emotional, or physical tension, strain, or distress. And everyone has stress in one form or another. Most jobs today—whether in the business world, in ministry, or as a "stay at home" wife and mother—have a certain amount of mental stress. Daily stress cannot be avoided, but at the end of the day we all need some quiet time to rest and rejuvenate. We must realize that proper rest and quiet time are vital to rebuilding the energies that have been expended. No wonder God established that we should work six days and then have a Sabbath—one day out of seven to totally rest from all our labors (see Exodus 20:8-10). Even God rested from His labors after six days of creation work (see Genesis 2:2).

We can handle normal stress, but when things get out of balance, we often sacrifice our good health. In today's world, more people feel bad than good. They are tired, worn out, and weary . . . with little or no energy. They cannot walk very far, and running is out of the question. Most are too tired to climb the stairs, and a simple thing like a sink full of dirty dishes can throw some into depression.

Medical science has come up with all kinds of names for this new batch of problems, but I think the root of much of it is the lack of peace that Jesus encouraged us to live in. The world itself is a stressful place. The noise levels are growing at an alarming rate. Years ago you could stop beside other cars at an intersection without worrying about the booming bass of a car stereo damaging your hearing. But today this scenario happens all the time, and the volume is enough to make a sane person want to scream. The sounds seem to be calling for the deepest rebellion hidden in our souls.

If your stress level is taking a toll on your health, happiness, and effectiveness, it's time to de-stress. ☺

Everybody is in a hurry—but sadly, many are going nowhere and they don't know it. All of this creates an atmosphere that is void of peace. The atmosphere is supercharged with strife and stress. Many families are experiencing pressure. Normal living frequently requires two incomes, thus both parents in a home have to work, or maybe the father works two jobs. Many single mothers work two or three jobs to pay the bills, and still have to do household chores at night.

Tired people in such circumstances succumb to temptation easier and get angry quicker than when they are rested. They are more impatient and more easily frustrated. It doesn't take a genius to recognize the plan of Satan. Remember, he plots and plans and lays his schemes. He plans your destruction, and he works his plan in deceptive ways that you may not recognize at first.

The demands and stresses on the lives of women today can sometimes be overwhelming, and the devil tries to take advantage of us when we are the most vulnerable. So if your stress level is taking a toll on your health, happiness, and effectiveness, it's time to de-stress before the devil drives you to distress.

You can do this by following the admonition found in Philippians 4:6,7: "Do not fret or have any anxiety about anything, but in every circumstance and in everything, by prayer and petition (definite requests), with thanksgiving, continue to make your wants known to God. And God's peace [shall be yours, that tranquil state of a soul assured of its salvation through Christ, and so fearing nothing from God and being content with its earthly lot of whatever sort that is, that peace] which transcends all understanding shall garrison and mount guard over your hearts and minds in Christ Jesus."

Now, that's the way to de-stress!

22

Don't Cry over Spilled Milk

$\mathcal{J}$esus spoke these encouraging words in John 14:27: "Peace I leave with you; My [own] peace I now give and bequeath to you. . . ." That is a wonderful confirmation that living in peace is the right of every Christian—even busy mothers who are sometimes tempted to cry—or explode—over spilled milk. I know because I've been there and done that.

I learned through some trying experiences that we can only walk in peace if we are willing to be adaptable and adjust to people and circumstances. When I lived in the "explode mode," it never failed that one of my children spilled something at the dinner table—every night. And every night I had a fit.

One of them would tip over a glass and immediately start crying as the milk was running across the table. I learned that when something is spilled, you have to try to get to it before it gets to the crack in the table, because milk will sour quickly in there with that other hidden dirt! And then eventually you will have to take the table apart and scrape dried milk and that other "mystery foods" out of its crevices with a table knife.

I used to shout at the kids, "Can't we ever have just one meal in peace?" I didn't realize that we could have had a meal in peace if I had stopped shouting at everyone. I could have brought peace to our table every night if I had just cleaned up and shut up.

So if you have wondered how to have peace, I can tell you that it will come if you will quit making a big deal about everything. You will have to be willing to let go of getting distraught over accidents or not getting your way.

One night I was under the table, because the milk the kids had spilled made it to the crack in the table before I could get to it, and it was running down the center table legs. I was having a fit, the kids were upset, and somebody kicked me in the head, which made me even madder. I knew it was an accident—that it hadn't been done on purpose—but that didn't seem to matter.

Poor Dave had to be weary of sitting down to dinner after working hard all day and having to endure my outbursts. (And I couldn't figure out why he wanted to go to the driving range every night and hit golf balls, so I'd throw a fit about that too.)

So there I was, under the table, cleaning up the mess and saying, "Every night somebody's got to spill something, and we just need some peace around here." And the Holy Ghost came to me—right under that table—and said, "Joyce, once the milk is spilled, no matter how big a fit you have, you are not going to get it to run back up the table legs, across the table, and back into the glass. You just need to learn how to go with the flow."

There are some things that we can do something about, but there are a whole lot of things that we can't do anything about. If it is something we can't do anything about, then we need to let it go and keep our joy. We need to hold our peace—and our tongues—do what is right, and let God work on our behalf.

When Jesus said, "Stop *allowing* yourselves to be agitated and disturbed; and do not *permit* yourselves to be . . . unsettled" (John 14:27, italics mine), He was saying that we must control ourselves.

For many years, I argued, "God, I don't want to act like that, but I just can't help it." Galatians 5:23 says that self-control is a fruit of the Spirit who dwells in us. We don't have to give way to unbridled emotions. God will give us power to do whatever we need to do, as often as we need it.

> *We need to hold our peace—and our tongues—do what is right, and let God work on our behalf.*

If you frequently lose your peace through emotional responses to life's trials, God can help you manage those emotions. Whether you need help with not getting upset over spilled milk or to forgive someone of an offense, the Lord will give you grace as often as you need it.

The only way to have peace is to let go of little offenses and irritations. Why not save some time and grief, and just forgive people right away? When you are upset, you are much less likely to be led by the Spirit of God. So quit crying over spilled milk, and allow the Spirit to help you maintain a quiet inner life. You will be a much happier woman . . . and those around you will be blessed as well.

23

Don't Set Yourself Up for Disappointment

*H*ave you ever been disappointed in someone because they failed to live up to your expectations of them? It is a common problem. We all have personal standards that we expect other people to meet, and we are disappointed when they fail to act the way we hoped. But is it really what they do that hurts us, or is it our own unrealistic expectations that set us up for the pain we feel when they don't perform to our standards?

God's Word tells us to expect things from Him, but not from other people. But how can we have relationships and not expect anything from people? In reality, there are some things we have a right to expect, but there are also expectations that we place on people that are not rightfully their responsibilities to fulfill. For example, my joy is not my husband's responsibility—although I thought it was for many years. If he wasn't doing what made me happy, I became angry. I thought he should be more concerned about my happiness and do things differently. It was *what I thought* that caused the problem, *not what he did.*

Dave and I have very few arguments now that I know my personal joy is my own responsibility, and not his. It is good for Dave to do things that make me happy, just as it is good for me to do things that please him, but I can tell you that there were many years in my life when it would have been practically impossible for anyone to keep me happy. My problems were in me. They were the result of abusive treatment in my childhood. I was filled with bitterness, resentment, rage, anger, and self-pity.

There was no way I could ever be truly happy until I dealt with those things. Dave could not deal with them—I had to do it. I was trying to place responsibility on Dave to make up for pain he had not caused. I was literally trying to punish him for the unfair abuse that someone else had perpetrated.

Over time, I noticed that no matter how badly I acted, Dave remained happy. It irritated me but also served as an example. I eventually became very hungry for the peace and joy I saw in his life, which were not dependent on any of his circumstances. In other words, he never made me responsible for his joy. If he had been dependent on me to make him happy, he would have never enjoyed life, because I gave him no reason to rejoice.

I believe that many wives try to make their husbands responsible for things that only they can do something about. If you are blaming your husband or someone else for your problems, you need to remember that Satan is your real enemy. We must take responsibility for ourselves, and stop expecting others to do for us what we should be doing for ourselves . . . or trusting God to do for us.

If I do a favor for someone with the expectation of receiving a similar favor in return, I am setting myself up for disappointment. The other person more than likely is unaware of my expectation, so it is unfair of me to become angry when they don't measure up.

We must take responsibility for ourselves, and stop expecting others to do for us what we should be doing for ourselves . . . or trusting God to do for us. ☺

The Bible tells us that when we give a gift, we are to expect nothing in return. It is God who returns to us what He wants us to have according to our investment and heart attitude (see Matthew 6:1-4).

We often think people should be able to read our minds when, in reality, we should be willing to clearly communicate what we expect from them. If I do a favor for someone with the expectation of receiving a favor in return, I need to let that person know by saying, "I am happy to do this-or-that for you, and I wonder if you would be willing to do thus-or-so for me?" That gets any expectations out in the open so nobody is left in the dark.

I can say to Dave, "Well, I expected you to stay home tonight." But if I hadn't communicated my desire to him ahead of time, it isn't fair to blame him later for something he didn't even know I wanted. I agree that some people should be more thoughtful than they are, but we should also be willing to ask for what we want and humble ourselves by being quick to forgive those who do not fulfill our wishes.

If you are a woman who truly wants to have peaceful relationships, I encourage you to examine yourself and ask God to reveal to you any unrealistic expectations you may have of other people.

We all have times when perhaps we have worked really hard or endured a difficult trial and need some special blessing to balance things out. I have learned over the years to ask God to give me encouragement when I need it. Sometimes He uses a person to do it, but I put my expectations in Him as my source, and not on people.

I ask God to provide encouragement when I feel that I have reached a place in life where I need something special to happen. I spent many years getting angry with people when I had times like this because I looked to them to make me feel better. It never produced anything but strife and offense. We must remember that people are not our source—God is.

Go to God, and if He wants to use people to bless you, He will; if not, trust that whatever He chooses is best for you at the present time. Don't set yourself up for disappointment—just trust God and His perfect timing.

24

Give God's Word
a Home in Your Heart

$\mathcal{I}$t seems that everyone needs answers about one thing or another in today's complicated world, and too often they seek answers and advice from unreliable sources instead of going to the most reliable source in the world—*The Holy Bible*.

Many people have not been taught about the Bible, and do not realize that it contains the answers to every question or need that may arise in life. Others know about the Bible, but because they have had limited exposure to its many truths, they are unaware that it contains some of the answers they desperately need.

For many years, I attended a church that gave me a great biblical foundation about salvation, but I learned very little beyond that. I had many problems in my life, but I wasn't getting victory over any of them. I certainly didn't know how to pursue the peace that I so desperately wanted.

I was not taught to study God's Word for myself, and because I didn't know the Word, I wasn't aware of the many deceptions that can grossly mislead people. For example, before I was in ministry, I worked at an office where a coworker studied astrology. She believed that the position of the planets and stars directed her life. At the time, the things she talked about seemed to make sense, and since I had no knowledge of what the Bible taught about the subject, I was ripe for the devil's deception. The things she talked about caught my attention, but, thank God, I didn't get involved in it.

Advice is easy to obtain from psychics, tarot card readers, sorcerers, and people skilled in divination who would like to run people's lives. They may give information that seems to make sense, but it will not produce lasting peace in a person's life. Such peace can only be found in a personal relationship with God and through the knowledge and wisdom found in the Holy Bible.

As I look back at those early years of being a believer, I am sad to say that nobody in my church told me not to follow these voices of deception. No one warned me that the Bible clearly says those who practice these types of things will not enter the kingdom of heaven (see Revelation 21:8). We are to follow God, not psychics, astrology, mediums, tarot card readers, or any such thing. God's Word actually says that these things are an abomination to Him. To enjoy peace, we must be led by the Lord of Peace.

Peace is our inheritance through Jesus, but unless we read His Word and learn how to appropriate it, we can miss out on what is rightfully ours. That is why giving the Word of God a home in our hearts is so important. By diligently studying the Word and hiding it in our hearts, we will know the truth, and we will discover true peace and satisfaction.

Colossians 3:15 teaches us that peace is to be the "umpire" in our lives, settling every issue that needs a decision. To gain and maintain peace in our hearts, we must make decisions based on what God's Word says.

Many people just go through life making decisions on their own, without consulting the most reliable resource book ever written—and too often their decisions bring heartache and trouble. But such an outcome can be avoided by seeking direction and guidance in the Bible and by allowing the peace of Christ to rule in our hearts.

To gain and maintain peace in our hearts, we must make decisions based on what God's Word says.

I encourage you to be a wise woman by giving God's Word a home in your heart. Consult it often and allow the presence of peace to help you decide and settle with finality all questions that arise in your mind. If you let the Word have its home in your heart and mind, it will give you insight, intelligence, and wisdom (see Colossians 3:16). You won't have to wonder, *Should I or shouldn't I?* The Word will be a lamp to your feet and a light to your path (see Psalm 119:105).

25

Learn to Be Wise with Your Words

Words are containers of power—either creative or destructive. What we say can tear down or build up . . . encourage or discourage. Psalm 19:14 says, "Let the words of my mouth and the meditation of my heart be acceptable in Your sight, O Lord, my [firm, impenetrable] Rock and my Redeemer." It is not acceptable to God when we use our mouths to bring hurt and destruction. Ephesians 4:29,30 teaches us not to grieve the Holy Spirit, and gives clear instructions concerning what grieves Him:

Let no foul or polluting language, nor evil word nor unwholesome or worthless talk [ever] come out of your mouth, but only such [speech] as is good and beneficial to the spiritual progress of others, as is fitting to the need and the occasion, that it may be a blessing and give grace (God's favor) to those who hear it. And do not grieve the Holy Spirit of God [do not offend or vex or sadden Him], by Whom you were sealed (marked, branded as God's own, secured) for the day of redemption (of final deliverance through Christ from evil and the consequences of sin).

As women, we have unique spheres of influence, and the Holy Spirit is the one who walks alongside us and encourages us in everything we do. His encouragement helps us become all that God designed us to be. We are to take His example and provide similar ministry for those in our little corner of the world.

People need to be encouraged! There is enough discouragement and negative feedback coming from the world. And we have the opportunity to operate on a higher system than that of the world.

With the Spirit of God as our Helper, we can be positive even in negative circumstances. We can believe in people that no one else would believe in. When we have the opportunity, love will help us to believe the best of every person and use our mouths to bring encouragement. Properly chosen words can actually change lives for the better.

Satan is fiercely attacking families today. And as women of God, we must not be a part of his evil plan. We must be careful that we don't wound family members by nagging them about their faults and thereby leaving an open door for the lies of the enemy. Of course, we must correct our children, and there are issues that must be confronted between marriage partners. But excessive faultfinding is ruining many relationships and bringing destruction to countless homes and lives. Faultfinding and criticism are spirits sent out from hell to bring destruction. The Word of God condemns faultfinding along with grumbling and complaining.

Just think of it, as women of God we can use our mouths and the power of our words to heal relationships or destroy them. James 3:5, 6 shows that major problems are birthed by wrong words: "Even so the tongue is a little member, and it can boast of great things. See how much wood or how great a forest a tiny spark can set ablaze! And the tongue is a fire. [The tongue is a] world of wickedness set among our members, contaminating and depraving the whole body and setting on fire the wheel of birth (the cycle of man's nature), being itself ignited by hell."

You may realize that some of the problems in your past relationships or circumstances have been ignited by wrong words that administered negative power. If so, it is unfortunate, but the good news is: *right words can affect your future in a positive way!* Find out what the Word of God has to say about His promises and what is available to you as a believer, and then *you can prophesy your future.* You have the privilege of

Properly chosen words can actually change lives for the better. ☺

calling "those things which be not as though they were" (Romans 4:17). You can take faith-filled words and reach out into the spiritual realm and begin to pull from God's storehouse the manifestation of those things that He has promised.

There are right and wrong uses of the mouth. Our mouths should belong to the Lord, and we should discipline what comes out of them. Matthew 15:11 states that it is not what goes into the mouth that defiles us, but what comes out of it. We should speak His words and use our mouths for His purposes.

Proverbs 4:24 says, "Put away from you false and dishonest speech, and willful and contrary talk put far from you." This Scripture instructs us to discipline our talking. Anything contrary to the Word of God should not be escaping our lips.

The Bible says that no man can tame the tongue. Therefore, we need abundant Holy Ghost help in order to have victory in this area. I recommend that you pray on a daily basis, "Lord, let the words of my mouth and the meditations of my heart be acceptable in your sight." And with the psalmist David, pray that God will guard your ways, that you may not sin with your tongue (see Psalm 39:1).

26

Lessons from the Silent Years Training Camp

As I have studied the Bible through the years, I have learned that most of the men and women whom God used greatly had to go through some silent years. These were periods of time in their lives when God seemed to hide them away while He worked in them and made changes in their characters that would be necessary for their future assignments. They entered into these periods of time one way and came out transformed.

It was no different for me. God had to deal with me, and it was painful. It took much longer than I expected or planned on, and it was much more painful than I would have ever thought I could endure.

It was exciting the day God called me into ministry, but I did not realize what I would have to go through in order to be prepared for the call. Had I known, I might not have said yes. I suppose this is why God hides certain things from us and gives us the grace for each of them as we go through them. There are some things we just don't need to know ahead of time. We only need to know that God has said He will never allow more to come upon us than we can bear.

I may look good to people now when I come out on the platform to minister to others, but you should have seen what I was like during the silent years, while I was being prepared for this ministry. I can tell you that it was not a pretty sight.

I certainly wasn't always a woman of faith. I experienced emotional ups and downs—lots of anger when things didn't go my way. It was very difficult for me to learn to be submissive to authority. I didn't start out with many of the fruits of the Spirit operating through me. The seed was in my spirit, but it had to be developed. We must always remember that gifts are given, but fruit must be developed.

We can have a gift that can take us somewhere but no character to keep us there if we don't submit to God's training camp.

Before I was on international radio and television, before many people knew who I was, I experienced "silent years," during which I had my dream and vision from God, but no big doors were opening for me. I had little opportunities, but I didn't have a little vision; therefore, most of the time I was frustrated and unthankful for what I was being allowed to do.

Oh, I needed a lot of changing and still do, but now I understand the process. I feel sorry for people who fight God all their lives, never understanding and accepting what He is really trying to do for them. We must trust God in the hard times. We must worship in the wilderness, not just the Promised Land. The Israelites worshiped God after they crossed the Red Sea and were safe. They sang and danced. They sang the right song but on the wrong side of the river. God wants to hear our praise *before* we experience victory.

I had years when the devil told me over and over that I was crazy, that I was not called by God and that I would make a fool of myself and fail. He assured me that nothing I did would bear good fruit. He told me that the suffering and pain would never end. He told me that I was a fool for believing in something that I could not see.

But God gave me grace to press on, and little by little I changed, "from glory to glory" (2 Corinthians 3:18 KJV), and as I did, things in my life also changed. I discovered that God releases to us what we are able to handle properly. Now I don't want anything that God doesn't want for me.

God wants to hear our praise before we experience victory. ☺

I have changed so much that sometimes I can barely remember what I used to be like. I know it was extremely unpleasant, but when the silent years were over, I was glad for the work that God had done in me by His grace. I didn't like them, nor did I understand them, but I would not be who I am or where I am today without them.

If you are experiencing some silent years in your life right now, I encourage you to recognize that this is God's training camp. He is building into your life exactly what is needed for you to be the anointed, powerful, and effective woman of God who can fulfill all that He has called you to do.

If you are troubled and upset about all the changes that need to be made in you, why not enter the rest of God? Struggling won't change you—neither will frustration and worry. But believing and trusting God and entering His rest during the process will make it easier. And the necessary changes will surely come.

So put yourself into God's hands and relax—the lessons you learn in the Silent Years Training Camp will transform you into a mighty woman of God who is equipped to make a difference for the kingdom of God.

27

You Can Be a Woman of Power

Far too many women today are fainthearted, weak in determination, and diseased with an "I can't" attitude—they are lacking in power. But it doesn't have to be that way. As God's child, you have been given the power, and all you need to do is recognize and then walk in that which is already yours.

Luke 10:19 says, "Behold! I have given you authority and power to trample upon serpents and scorpions, and [physical and mental strength and ability] over all the power that the enemy [possesses]; and nothing shall in any way harm you."

Now, that's good news! We can receive everything that God has provided in Jesus Christ through faith. It is very important to constantly believe that we have power, and we do that by developing and maintaining a "power consciousness." Satan wants us to feel weak and believe that as women, we are incapable and unable to be powerful. He wants us to believe and apply the lie that we "can't" to every aspect of our lives.

But if we take an aggressive stand against the devil by coming back at him using the Word of God as a weapon, we can shut him down. First Peter 5:9 says we are to "withstand him; be firm in faith [against his onset—rooted, established, strong, immovable, and determined] . . . ."

I received a letter from a woman recently who told me that "resisting the devil at his onset" was one of the most valuable things she had ever learned from me. I think that all too often we wait to see how bad the problem will get before we do anything about it. We finally decide to address the issue after we are entrenched so deeply that it is very difficult to get out.

But God has given us spiritual power for spiritual warfare—aggression that goes beyond the physical or natural realm. This power is an effective weapon in the realm of the spirit. We must resist the enemy by refusing to give up no matter how difficult the fight may be. Spiritual power is released when our faith is firm. The woman who walks in faith will approach every situation with an attitude of enemy-conquering faith!

Try approaching every situation in your life (no matter how large or small) with a simple, childlike faith—believing that God is good and that He has a good plan for your life. And remember that He is working in your situation right now. Just because we can't see the outcome yet doesn't mean He isn't secretly working behind the scene.

God often uses His creative powers in secret. Just think of all the miraculous work that is going on inside a mother's womb when she is expecting the birth of a child. The womb is a secret place where the eye cannot see, but when it is God's time for the birth, He brings forth the miracle! It is the same with many of our circumstances. God is working, and when we faithfully believe in His mighty power, the miracle comes in His perfect timing.

An attitude of confidence will exude from the woman who knows who she is in Christ and believes in the power that the Bible says is hers through faith. When we develop a power consciousness, we can approach God's throne boldly (see Hebrews 4:16), and pray aggressively. Ephesians 3:20 tells us that God can do more than we dare to hope, ask, or think. We should be spiritually daring in our prayers.

> *The woman who walks in faith will approach every situation with an attitude of enemy-conquering faith!*

I boldly pray for things that I know I don't deserve, but I step out in faith, believing in God's mercy and goodness. I believe that He will bless me because He is good, not because I am.

Be an aggressive woman of God. *Have an aggressive voice*, speaking positively, definitely, clearly, and confidently. Speak with power—put some energy in your voice. *Be an aggressive giver.* Don't give the least amount, but consider what you could comfortably give and then purposely give a little more. *Work aggressively.* Don't dread your daily jobs—attack your work with an attitude that says, "I am going to conquer this project!" And most importantly, *love aggressively.* Love is a choice, not a feeling. It is a decision you must make every day. It is an effort, and it will cost you something, but you have the power to do it, and the rewards are magnificent. You will be a woman of faith and power who not only confidently enjoys life every day, but you will be a wonderful witness to others of the power and goodness of God.

28

You Are a Righteous Woman!

Are you aware of Who you are? According to God's Word, you are the righteousness of God in Christ Jesus. Second Corinthians 5:21 tells us that, "For our sake He made Christ [virtually] to be sin Who knew no sin, so that in and through Him we might become [endued with, viewed as being in, and examples of] the righteousness of God [what we ought to be, approved and acceptable and in right relationship with Him, by His goodness]." Righteous, perfected, and complete. Does that sound like a description of you?

If you find this difficult to believe, I am reminding you that whatever God says is true, and He says that you are a woman who is perfected and complete in Him. When you start to believe that, you will no longer feel that you are lacking anything or that there is anything wrong with you.

John 3:16 says, "For God so greatly loved and dearly prized the world that He [even] gave up His only begotten (unique) Son, so that whoever believes in (trusts in, clings to, relies on) Him shall not perish (come to destruction, be lost) but have eternal (everlasting) life." Are you a "whoever"? Please notice that there are no special requirements. The Word says, "whoever believes."

Like me, you may have spent enough years of your life in struggles and vain works of the flesh. The Lord showed me one day that I had spent my life trying to get in a chair I was already sitting in. Think how frustrating it would be to struggle to get somewhere you already were, and how freeing to discover you were there and could stop struggling. This is where we come into the rest of God mentioned in

Hebrews 4. I had been trying to be righteous or acceptable to God through my works, and I was already made righteous and acceptable through Jesus. Ephesians 1:6 tells us that we are made acceptable in the beloved. I love that!

This helps us to understand why the Gospel is referred to as good news. Isn't it good news that your acceptability to God is not based on your performance, but on your believing in His performance? Jesus was perfect for you and me. He suffered and died in our place and paid the debt we owed.

We need to learn to identify with the substitutionary work of Jesus. A *substitute* is "someone or something that takes the place of another." To *identify with* means "to relate to, or the transferal of response to an object regarded as identical to another."

For example, let's say your child breaks a neighbor's window and the angry neighbor is rightfully angry with the child. However, he realizes that the child has no ability to make it right, so he transfers his anger to you as the child's parent, who pays for the damage. And because the parent takes the place of the child, the neighbor is no longer angry. This is good news, and it is exactly what God has done for us in Christ.

When we break God's laws, He is rightfully angry, and we owe a debt. However, God realizes that we have no ability to pay the debt or to keep His law perfectly. So He goes to Jesus, who takes care of it for us. And because of that, our fellowship with God is restored. Wow! This takes time to ponder. Some things are so good that we just can't take them in right away!

Many women are having an identity crisis. They simply do not know who they are in Christ. They are identifying with their sins, failures, and comparisons with other women, and their own ability to fix themselves rather than identifying with Christ and His substitutionary work on the cross.

According to God's Word, you are the righteousness of God in Christ Jesus. ☙

Believe what the Word says about

you and start enjoying the life that Jesus provided. We honor God when we believe His Word above what we think or feel. I like to meditate on 2 Corinthians 5:17 NKJV, which says, "If anyone is in Christ, he is a new creation; old things have passed away; behold, all things have become new."

Let this be a new day in which you begin to see yourself in a new way. Look through the eyes of faith and see as a little child. God is waiting with open arms.

29

Hope for the Lonely Woman

Many women in today's world are lonely. Even those who have others around them often say they are lonely. The death of a spouse or another close loved one can leave you lonely and confused as well as feeling abandoned. However, your circumstances don't have to be quite so severe to put you into the category of lonely.

Perhaps you have moved to a new neighborhood in a new city, have begun attending a new church, or have just started a new job, and you just don't seem to fit in yet. I know what it's like to be lonely.

For years the devil convinced me that no one liked me. I believed that, and I received what I believed. I did not like myself, and so I believed that no one else could like me either. Learning to like myself and to pray for favor has changed my life, and it will change yours. Social "poverty" is not part of our heritage from the Lord.

Beware of being passive. Don't just wait for someone to fall into your life before you are willing to have fellowship. Find someone who is lonelier than you and be a blessing to them. Giving always brings joy into your life. Be friendly and pleasant and you'll attract others who are also friendly and pleasant to be around.

Many women feel that life is more painful than they can bear. If that is true of you, I encourage you to remember Jesus in the Garden of Gethsemane. John the Baptist, the closest person to Him, and the only one who really understood His ministry, had been violently murdered. All of Jesus' friends

Time has healing properties, and will eventually bring new direction to your life.

had disappointed Him. He had ministered to them for three years, and now He needed them to spend only one final hour with Him, and they hadn't been able to stay awake.

Luke 22:44 records that Jesus was under such intense pressure in His mind that His sweat became like great drops of blood. I believe as you realize that Jesus does indeed know how you feel and has promised never to leave you nor forsake you, that you will be strengthened to press on.

Things are always changing, and the way you feel right now will change with time. Time has healing properties, and will eventually bring new direction to your life.

I also believe that lonely women can learn to enjoy being alone. There is a major difference between being lonely and being alone. There is also a difference in being alone and being bored. There is no need for you to live a life of boredom. There are far too many people who need help for anyone to be bored. You may see yourself as a needy woman, but you should see yourself as a woman who can meet needs. As you reach out to others, you will be sowing seed for your own loneliness to be overcome.

God has a good plan for your life. "For I know the thoughts and plans that I have for you, says the Lord, thoughts and plans for welfare and peace and not for evil, to give you hope in your final outcome" (Jeremiah 29:11). Be encouraged by this Scripture. Also choose to take some God-inspired action now. This can be a new beginning for you!

30

Don't Let Satan Steal Your Future

$\mathcal{G}$ can't help noticing how often I hear women blaming something or somebody else for the mess they find themselves in, when much of the time they are in a negative situation because of wrong choices they've made in the past. We reap the benefits of wisdom when we make right choices. But if we do foolish things, we will reap the consequences of foolishness. Proverbs 19:3 says, "The foolishness of man subverts his way [ruins his affairs]. . . ."

I know of only one way to overcome the results of a series of bad decisions, and that is through a series of good ones. We are free to choose what we think, what we do, whom we want to be around, and many other things. Freedom of choice is wonderful, of course. Thank God, He has given us the privilege of making our own choices. However, there are some responsibilities involved with freedom of choice.

Too many women want their lives to change, but they don't want to change their lifestyles. Christianity is a lifestyle, and it begins with a prayer of commitment to Jesus Christ. Then as we increase in the knowledge of the truth of God's Word, we're able to confidently make good decisions about our future. I would so like to see women begin to understand the need to pray for a tender conscience so we can maintain a godly standard in our lives that gives hope to women everywhere. Christianity must become a lifestyle for women. Period.

God wants us to believe His promises because that's what will bring them to pass in our lives. $\backsim$

The Bible says we are to put all of our

confidence in Christ. We are anointed, and God promises to lead and guide us. Isaiah 30:21 says, "And your ears will hear a word behind you, saying, This is the way; walk in it, when you turn to the right hand and when you turn to the left." We must learn to pay close attention and be sensitive to God. Isaiah goes on to say in chapter 45:2, "I will go before you and level the mountains [to make the crooked places straight]; I will break in pieces the doors of bronze and cut asunder the bars of iron." No doubt about it, Satan has laid a crooked path before us. But God wants us to believe His promises because that's what will bring them to pass in our lives.

"Prize Wisdom highly and exalt her, and . . . she will bring you to honor when you embrace her . . . I have taught you in the way of skillful and godly Wisdom [which is comprehensive insight into the ways and purposes of God]; I have led you in paths of uprightness. When you walk, your steps shall not be hampered [your path will be clear and open]; and when you run, you shall not stumble" (Proverbs 4:8,11,12).

Having a deep understanding of the ways and purposes of God is my definition of wisdom. Your path will be clear and open when you walk in wisdom. The Word tells us that Jesus has been made unto us wisdom (see 1 Corinthians 1:30). If Jesus lives in you, then His wisdom is ever present—constantly available to you. When you are faced with making a difficult decision, wisdom stands right beside you crying out, "Listen to me. Don't do what you feel like doing or say whatever you feel like saying. Follow God and His Word. It is the beginning of wisdom."

Perhaps you have made some bad choices. Don't mourn and grieve over them. It's time to choose wisdom and start living a victorious life that Satan cannot steal from you. Walking in victory doesn't mean you'll have a problem-free future, but it does mean that when problems come, you'll be able to handle them by making right choices. Don't let Satan steal your future! You can become a woman who makes right choices . . . starting today. I urge you to turn yourself and all your situations over to God. His blessings are waiting for you!

31

Women and Motives

God started dealing with me about motives many years ago when I was just starting out in ministry. This was a new lesson for me. I was a worker. I was always busy with some kind of project, and much of my work involved church activities that would have been considered "good deeds." As God began to dig deeper into the *why behind the what*, I started realizing that much of what I did looked as if it was for others—but in reality, it was for me. It made me look good . . . made me feel good about myself. It caused me to have favor with "the right people."

I learned that a great deal of what I was doing was not done in obedience to God. I was a man pleaser. I did a lot of things because others thought I should or expected me to. All of this "new truth" felt as if it was wrecking my life, especially when God got the point across that He did not want me doing anything unless my motive was pure.

Over a short period of time, I submitted to God and had pure motives, but it did not happen quickly. I can definitely say that I changed from glory to glory, little by little. It takes a long time to become honest enough with ourselves to face the truth about our motives. Then it takes even more time to be willing to let go of our old ways.

Jeremiah 17:9 provides some insight into how difficult it is to truly know oneself. "The heart is deceitful above all things, and it is exceedingly perverse and corrupt and severely, mortally sick! Who can know it [perceive, understand, be acquainted with his own heart and mind]?"

It is relatively easy for women to deceive themselves. When we want or don't want something, our minds and emotions join in with our already determined will to aid the flesh in getting its own way. Unless a woman is sincerely willing to walk in the Spirit—to follow after God's will instead of her own—it is not difficult to make excuses for the lack of peace or the sensing that something is not right.

I look back now and realize that in many of my "works of the flesh," God was attempting to let me know that my motives were not right—that my works were not pleasing to Him because they were not being done out of a pure heart. At the time, though, I wanted to do what I was doing so intensely that I wouldn't be still long enough to find out if God was really convicting me. I was afraid that He might tell me not to do it—and to avoid facing that, I deceived myself into thinking what I was feeling was the devil, or my imagination.

How about you? How pure are your motives? Colossians 3:15 says we should follow after peace and let peace be the umpire in our lives. Peace should decide if something is in or out—not a fleshly peace (because the flesh is getting its own way) but a deep peace that only God can give. His peace is His approval.

Take a look at why you are doing things. Don't live in a whirlwind of doing, never stopping to ask if the works are really pleasing to God. Many women do things because other people want or expect them to. They do things out of fear of losing their friends, or of being judged critically. This was a difficult lesson for me to learn. I wanted acceptance, but I quickly found that I could not be a people pleaser and a God pleaser. If I did something just because my friends were pushing me to—even though I knew deep inside that God didn't want me involved in it—my motives were impure, and God was not pleased.

The heart is deceitful above all things, and it is exceedingly perverse and corrupt and severely, mortally sick! ☺

I firmly believe that Jesus is worthy of having women serve Him who have pure hearts. Personally, I feel this is something I can attempt to do to honor Him. My flesh may not like it but my spirit rejoices. There is a price to pay but the rewards are rich. God is an investor. He was willing to pay the price to redeem His own. Are we willing to pay the price to have purity in our lives—purity of motives, thoughts, attitudes, words, and actions? Remember, Matthew 5:8 promises that the pure in heart will be blessed, for they shall see God.

32

The Beauty of Submission

I can almost hear you now. *What in the world could Joyce be thinking by titling this story "The Beauty of Submission"?* Woman to woman . . . just between us girls, the subject of submission is never a favorite topic, whether it's in the marriage relationship, the parent-child relationship, or the employer-employee relationship. Even in the church, it has often been misunderstood and sometimes used as an excuse for manipulation, control, and even abuse.

Still, God set up everything in the universe on the basis of authority and submission to that authority. What was His purpose in doing that? Why did God give Adam and Eve liberty to eat from every tree in the garden except one? I believe His goal in forbidding them to dine on the fruit of that one tree was to teach them obedience. There is no way to learn obedience apart from a set standard of limitations.

I don't know of any born-again, Holy Spirit-filled woman who doesn't want to operate in the authority the Bible teaches that she has been given. Yet, we actually witness very few functioning in it. Why? Could it be that many have failed to learn how to submit to *natural* authority? Until we know how to come under natural authority, we will not operate in *spiritual* authority.

There is no way to learn obedience apart from a set standard of limitations. ⌒

Everyday life offers us opportunities in which submission to natural authority surfaces. Obviously, one that is uppermost in the minds of most women is in the marriage relationship. The Word addresses the issue of marital submission throughout the New Testament. For example, "Be subject to one another out of reverence for Christ (the Messiah, the Anointed One). Wives, be subject (be submissive and adapt yourselves) to your own husbands as [a service] to the Lord. For the husband is head of the wife as Christ is the Head of the church, Himself the Savior of [His] body" (Ephesians 5:21-23).

My husband, Dave, is anointed to be the head of our family, and the anointing flows down from the head. If I have a negative attitude toward Dave, and I'm not in agreement with him, the anointing that is upon him will not flow down to me. If I continue to be disagreeable and negative, this struggle in our relationship can affect other family matters. However, if I stay under Dave's covering, God can bring an answer to these matters and they can be handled with ease.

This cannot happen, however, without my willingness to be obedient to the Holy Spirit. To live in harmony, we must forgive quickly and frequently. We must not be easily offended. We should be generous in mercy and patience. We cannot be self-seeking, and that is where humility comes in. It takes humility to have a correct response to authority.

Humble women get the help! First Peter 5:6 exhorts, "Therefore humble yourselves [demote, lower yourselves in your own estimation] under the mighty hand of God, that in due time He may exalt you." As Christian women, we should have a humble attitude, knowing that apart from Him, we can do nothing (see John 15:5). Our flesh wants to be independent, and God insists on total dependence on Him.

Following His direction ushers in victory. Ignoring it brings defeat. The Word of God is very clear about submission in marriage. Yet the majority of marriages are in trouble today. Why? Clearly, we're not following His instructions. A husband who really loves his wife has a responsibility to be the head of his wife as Christ is the Head of the church. Husbands must take their position as high priest of their homes. They should follow God, and their family should follow them.

Although we are to properly submit to authority in our lives, ungodly control must be confronted and rejected. Allowing others to control us makes us as guilty as they are. A Christian woman who is being abused by her spouse, for example, needs to understand that there are significant differences between submission and abuse. Nobody volunteers to be abused by anyone.

It is also important that we avoid trying to be the Holy Spirit in people's lives by giving them direction that is coming from us rather than from God. Don't allow yourself to be controlled, but don't become a controller either. For years, I literally threw a fit every time I did not get my way. When I could not control what was taking place, I wasn't happy. Obviously, God had to deal with that fleshly attitude in me. Until I learned not to be a controller, it seemed He continually placed me in situations that I could not control, with people I could not control. I had to learn to come under His divine control.

We need to pray for our husbands and others who are in positions of authority over us! Picture what could happen if a wife—instead of calling all her friends to complain about her husband—prayed for God to radically and outrageously bless him? What if she prayed for him to become more loving, affectionate, and sympathetic every day—even when he comes home tired, grouchy, and unreasonable? Imagine all those negatives turning into some powerful positives!

If we are trusting God to bless us through those who are in authority over us, yet we aren't praying for them—it's as if we're not praying for ourselves. James 5:16 says, "The earnest (heartfelt, continued) prayer of a righteous man makes tremendous power available [dynamic in its working]." Just think of it—tremendous power is made available when we pray! Imagine the peace and contentment we would enjoy in our lives if we were to consistently pray for blessing to abound toward the people God has placed in authority over us!

Although we are to properly submit to authority in our lives, ungodly control must be confronted and rejected.

In the workplace, picture what could

happen if we prayed for the boss instead of murmuring, faultfinding, and complaining about him or her, the way the company is run, or how underpaid we think we are! What if our prayers resulted in the boss being so blessed that he or she became a happier, more contented person . . . and all that happiness and contentment filtered down to you and others? What glorious, joy-filled lives we could have if we were to live as Jesus instructed.

I believe there is beauty in godly submission and it is vitally important—not only for you, but for those with whom you are in a relationship. Just as children learn that they must trust us and follow our instructions, so we need to trust God and follow His instructions. His Word instructs, encourages, and urges believers to live in peace because God wants us to have blessed and powerful lives. Jesus came that we might have and enjoy life (see John 10:10). I am determined to follow His instructions, submit cheerfully, operate in authority mercifully, and enjoy my life as a blood-bought woman of God. How about you?

33

Healing for Your Broken Heart

Isaiah 61:1 says that Jesus heals the brokenhearted. Coming from a background of abuse and relationships with dysfunctional people, I know firsthand what it means to need Jesus to "restore my soul." I was rebellious, controlling, manipulative, harsh, judgmental, and very negative. I continually worried and was very unstable emotionally. I was in a good mood when I got my way and in a foul mood when I did not.

Jesus healed my broken heart and my wounded personality. I suspect that you have suffered hurts and wounds that have kept you back and held you captive. You don't want to be difficult to get along with, but your personality, like mine, may have been altered by tragedies and abuse until it seems as though you've lost yourself. You may be wearing so many masks and playing so many parts that you don't really know what you're supposed to be like anymore.

I know how you feel. I was imprisoned inside a bleeding, wounded soul. I had built walls of fear and distrust, designed to keep people from hurting me more. But these shielding walls also kept me a prisoner, isolated and alone.

I didn't realize that Jesus had opened the prison doors. The Word says He came to " . . . bind up and heal the brokenhearted, to proclaim liberty to the [physical and spiritual] captives and the opening of the prison and of the eyes to those who are bound" (Isaiah 61:1).

I began to experience emotional healing and deliverance from the many bondages I had in my life as I received the truth of God's Word and began to understand that I did not have to be trapped in my past. We can't get beyond what we believe. Whatever we believe is the way it is for us. Even if we believe lies, we are prisoners to those lies. Why do you believe what you believe? Romans 12:2 teaches us that the mind must be completely renewed. Only then do we experience God's prearranged plan for our lives—and His plan is always the best plan for us.

Satan is a liar who starts early trying to construct a stronghold in our mind. Strongholds develop when believing Satan's lies deceives us. Soon we are trapped in a maze of lies. The only way out is for our mind to be renewed by the Word of God, but finding a new way of living requires finding a new way of thinking!

I did not believe God loved me, so I was not receiving His love. It was available to me, but I had so many fears—especially of what people thought of me. I also experienced much fear concerning my relationship with God, which caused me to live very legalistically. I served the Lord under the Law instead of being led by His Holy Spirit. My Christian walk was draining me rather than energizing me. I was laboring and I didn't even know why.

You may recognize some of the same pain you've been feeling as you read my description of the hurts I suffered in the past. Well, I have good news for you! Jesus wants to do a complete work of restoration in your life. He wants to heal your broken heart, your emotions, your mind, and your will. He wants you to experience every good thing He has planned for you.

I urge you to ask the Lord to take your hand and lead you out of those prison doors that He is holding open for you to walk through. Ask Him to cleanse your heart of all bitterness, resentment, and unforgiveness. God wants to do a new thing in you! He cares about every part of you. He has paid the price to redeem you. Allow Him to give back to you all that the enemy has stolen, and more besides.

Finding a new way of living requires finding a new way of thinking! ☺

Let go of your laboring and become an inheritor! Your inheritance is righteousness, peace, and joy in the Holy Ghost. Isn't it time for you to spend your inheritance and begin to enjoy a quality of life such as God Himself enjoys? Press on!

34

Emotional Stability 101

One of the primary objectives in the life of a successful Christian woman, I believe, should be emotional stability—the ability to be emotionally stable in any given situation. "He who is slow to anger is better than the mighty," the writer of Proverbs says, "he who rules his [own] spirit than he who takes a city" (Proverbs 16:32). We are women, after all, and we experience a wide range of emotions, but an emotional roller coaster is a really hard place for any woman to live. In order to get our emotions to level out we must make a quality decision that we are not going to live by feelings.

My husband, Dave, has always been very stable emotionally. If anyone began to talk negatively about us, I would get nervous and Dave would say, "We don't have the problem; the people who are talking about us do. Our hearts are right before God, so why should we be bothered? Let's just relax and trust the Lord to handle everything."

Dave's steadfast, unchanging character reminds me of a rock, which is one of the names given to Jesus (see 1 Corinthians 10:4). Jesus is called the Rock because He is solid and stable, "[always] the same, yesterday, today, [yes] and forever" (Hebrews 13:8). Jesus did not allow Himself to be moved or led around by His emotions even though He was subject to the same feelings that we are. Instead, He chose to be led by the Spirit.

I wanted to be more like Dave, who was more like Jesus than I was. Dave says he can remember years ago when he would drive home from work in the evening, thinking, *I wonder what Joyce will be like tonight? Will she be happy or angry, talkative or quiet, in a good mood or a bad mood?* How he left me in the morning might not be how he found me in the evening. My soul rather than my spirit controlled me, because my mind was not yet renewed by studying God's Word.

I was addicted to excitement, for example. I found it difficult to settle down and live an ordinary, everyday life—relaxing and enjoying my husband, my children, and the home God had given me. I had to have something exciting going on all the time. And I'm not saying it's wrong to be excited, but it is dangerous to be excessive.

Women need to be careful about becoming all "hyped up" about things, because very often hype leads to disappointment. I'll give you an illustration to make my point. I would get all worked up about going on vacation. If it got postponed or didn't turn out the way I expected, I would experience a very emotional low.

It would have been better for me (and my entire family) to view things with a calm delight than to build them up in my mind. Jesus said in John 15:11 that He wanted His joy—meaning calm delight—to be in us, complete and overflowing.

These days I still get excited about planning a vacation, but I don't swing from the chandeliers over it. I maintain a calm delight, and I don't allow my emotions to get hyped up and attached to great expectations. That way, if things don't turn out the way I thought, I won't have an emotional crash.

I'm talking about balance here. If you have been the type of woman (as I once was) who was careful not to have any expectations at all so I'd never be disappointed, I'm here to tell you that isn't a reasonable position to take either. It's just that every single day is not going to be gloriously exciting. There will be days when God brings excitement into our lives, but we cannot spend the majority of our lives seeking excitement. In Psalm 143:10, David said, "Let Your good Spirit lead me into a level country."

In Psalm 143:10, David said, "Let Your good Spirit lead me into a level country." ☺

I love that Psalm. Don't you want your mind to live in a level country? I know that I do. You are probably thinking, *I have this same problem, Joyce, but how can I change?* You have to be willing to let your flesh suffer when you choose what you know is right. You can't deny the existence of your feelings. Instead, you need to channel them in the right direction, finding the place of balance that brings peace. It's a lesson taken from what I call "Emotional Stability 101." That means it's the first in a series of steps that we must take to keep our emotions under control.

Allowing the flesh to suffer while its power over us is weakening is not pleasant, but it is impossible to see God's glory without it. Romans 8:16,17 says, "The Spirit Himself [thus] testifies together with our own spirit, [assuring us] that we are children of God. And if we are [His] children, then we are [His] heirs also: heirs of God and fellow heirs with Christ [sharing His inheritance with Him]; only we must share His suffering if we are to share His glory."

As I grew in my relationship with the Lord over the years and gained knowledge of His Word, I started being convicted in my heart that I was behaving badly. I had a choice to make at that point: either to keep acting in a way I knew was not pleasing to God (and was, in fact, hurting my family), or to do what I knew Jesus would do, even though my flesh was screaming and pressuring me to continue letting it be in control. How about you? How are your roller-coaster emotions affecting those you love?

God does not expect you to be perfect. He just wants you to keep moving toward Him, aligning your will with His and letting Him develop the fruit of self-control in you. Having emotions is not a sin—it's what we do with them that matters. Submit yourself to God, and any situation that causes your emotions to dictate how you act, and choose to refuse to give in to them. Ask God to help you remain stable. He will give you the ability to be calm in your day of adversity (see Psalm 94:13). He loves you! He desires to do a work in you and your circumstances as long as you are determined to walk in emotional stability.

Having emotions is not a sin—it's what we do with them that matters. ☺

35

Are You Letting Your Light Shine?

*T*he decline of commitment to excellence in these last days coupled with the increase of mediocrity that results from a lack of integrity adds up to an all-time low in the world's standard of values. Isaiah prophesied about society's decline in the last days: "For behold, darkness shall cover the earth, and dense darkness [all] peoples . . . " (Isaiah 60:2). Jesus himself said, "And then many will be offended and repelled and will . . . betray one another and pursue one another with hatred" (Matthew 24:10).

We live in a world that does not honor God and has little concern for moral or ethical integrity. Quantity is preferred over quality, and few people seem to care who gets stepped on or what gets left behind in pursuit of their perception of happiness and success. But there is good news. Many places in the Bible say that though we are in the world, we do not have to be of the world. Women who are believers don't belong to this world, but we are to be a light in it. Are you a light in your world? Where do you start?

Integrity is defined as "a firm adherence to a code or standard of values; the state of being unimpaired; soundness; the quality or condition of being undivided: completeness." Our standards as Christian women should be much higher than the world's.

Ask yourself some of these questions: Would you rob a bank? Would you speak ugly gossip about a sister in the Lord? Would you lie to your children or to your friends? Do you ever sign up

> *We live in a world that does not honor God and has little concern for moral or ethical integrity.*

to work in the church nursery and not show up? Do you exaggerate to make a story sound better?

Did you answer "yes" to any of these inquiries? Granted, most of us wouldn't even think of robbing a bank. But how many of us do compromise on things that we consider to be of lesser or minimal importance—things that Jesus, our standard of integrity, wouldn't do? We must not drift toward the way of the world.

Integrity is being committed to a life of excellence. Our God is excellent. We must be committed to excellence if we are to represent Him to the world. Matthew 5:41 says to go the extra mile—don't just do what you have to do. *Excellence* means "to surpass or be exceptionally better; to go beyond." I believe the Lord has caused me to know that real excellence is to do the more excellent thing even when nobody is looking—even when nobody is around to reward us, notice us, or recognize us as exceptional women.

Integrity is keeping your word even if it costs you something. Psalm 15:4 says to swear to your own hurt and do not change. When you make a commitment, you need to follow through and do what you said you would.

It's easier to keep commitments when you have spent time counting the cost before you commit to do something. Think it through thoroughly. Are you able to see it through to the finish? Don't say "yes" with your mouth, until you know in your heart that you will be able to back up your words with action. When your conscience says "no," don't do it!

Be a woman of excellence. Make integrity a habit. Proverbs 20:7 says, "The righteous man (or woman) walks in his integrity; blessed (happy, fortunate, enviable) are his children after him." The seed of your integrity can even produce happy, fortunate children who are to be envied! As God's representatives, Christian women are called to show the world what He is like. Remember: The world is not reading their Bibles. They're reading you and me!

Remember: The world is not reading their Bibles. They're reading you and me! ☺

36

Do You Play the "Blame Game"?

Just like Adam and Eve, we often use excuses to play the "blame game" as a means of escaping responsibility, avoiding difficult situations, and hard-to-like people. When Adam and Eve sinned, the first thing they did was to run and hide from God. When God confronted him, Adam said, "The woman whom You gave to be with me—she gave me [fruit] from the tree, and I ate. And the Lord God said to the woman, What is this you have done? And the woman said, The serpent beguiled (cheated, outwitted, and deceived) me, and I ate" (Genesis 3:12, 13). Both of them blamed someone else for what they had done.

But God's nature is to confront issues and deal with them. We never win a victory by running away from our responsibilities. Do you find yourself coming up with unnecessary excuses for things? Do you place blame for things you've done on someone else . . . or even on God? We usually end up in trouble when we try to run from things—from God, places, people, or situations. I have learned that God usually sends me right back to where I ran from, and I start making progress again at that point. Take Hagar for example.

Hagar was an Old Testament woman who didn't really have a very nice life. She was an Egyptian servant girl in the house of Abram and Sarai. The couple had no children, so Sarai gave her to Abram to be his second wife in order to produce the family Sarai desperately wanted but seemed unable to have. When Hagar became pregnant, she also became proud and arrogant toward Sarai. After all, she'd accomplished something her mistress wasn't able to do. Do you know any women like Hagar? Well, Sarai got pretty upset about

Hagar's pregnancy, and in verse 6 of Genesis chapter 16, we find that Sarai was so upset that she mistreated Hagar and Hagar ran away.

In Genesis 16:9, we find that God has sent an angel of the Lord to find Hagar and send her right back to where she'd come from—even to face the wrath of her angry mistress. She ran from a difficult situation, but God sent her back. Why? God wants us to face our issues and deal with them. He does not want us to run and hide.

Women run from many things—even things like losing weight. We start out all right, but when we get uncomfortably hungry, we run from the discipline of dieting and run toward the refrigerator. We run from uncomfortable relationships, marriages, difficult jobs, people who are hard to get along with, challenges that require endurance, and all sorts of things.

It's time to face reality. Life is not always easy, but God is always on our side. Women of God are just as anointed to handle difficult things as easy ones. God did not fill us with His Holy Spirit so we can quit when the going gets rough, but He strengthens us to complete our course. Now I know there are certain situations from which we must get away for our own safety and sanity, but I believe they are few compared to all the things women are running from.

Have you been running from facing the truth about some important issues in your life? Perhaps it's time to take an inventory. Just check to see if you are running from the past, the future, difficult people, your own weaknesses, a hard task, losing weight, getting out of debt—all things that are unpleasant, yes, but need to be dealt with.

One of the things that will put you over during a time of trial and

Have you been running from facing the truth about some important issues in your life? ☺

testing is recalling things God has already done for you. You'll begin to realize that if He's brought you this far, He can take you the rest of the way. I encourage you to confront difficult situations in the power of the Holy Spirit and see your life change for the better.

37

There Is Potential
for Greatness in You!

$\mathcal{I}$ am convinced that most women have potential for greatness, but just having potential is not enough unless you are willing to take a risk, step out, and let God go to work in your life. The word *potential* is defined as "existing in possibility but not in actuality; powerful but not in use."

Having potential doesn't necessarily mean that it is positively going to happen. It just means that it *can* happen if we add the other right "ingredients" along with it. For instance, if I have a cake mix on the shelf in my kitchen, then I have the potential of having a cake. But just because that cake mix is on my shelf doesn't guarantee that I am going to have cake. There are some things I must do to get it from a mix on the shelf to a cake on the table.

It's the same with us. We have potential because God places gifts and talents in us, but they must be developed. Remember when camera film had to be taken to a processor for development? Before the days of digital cameras, Dave and I used to take a lot of pictures and then put off getting them developed. We had rolls of film lying around and didn't even remember what was on them. Just having the undeveloped film does us no good at all. Unless we get the pictures developed, we have wasted our time and money.

Many women today are wasting their potential because they are not developing what God has placed in them. Instead of developing what they have, they worry about what they don't have, and their potential just goes down the tubes. They might have been world changers!

You can make a difference in someone's life if you will develop what you have. But it takes time, determination, and hard work to develop potential into the manifestation of that potential.

Many years ago God began to show me that I had the potential to help other women. Now my life is manifesting that potential through my ministry that brings hope and healing to many hurting people—especially women. I have a concern for women, and I want to help them. I especially want to see them be all that God wants them to be.

We live in a very impatient world. Everyone seems to have a "drive-through" mentality. They don't want to take the time to let things develop because they want everything right now. Does this sound like anyone you know? You can have a "drive-through" mentality, but it won't lead to "drive-through" maturity. It's impossible. You must walk it out and let God do something on the inside of you.

Unfortunately, too many women with God-given potential give up too easily. A lot of women have *wishbone*, but a bone density test might reveal that they're short on *backbone*. I can tell you that wishbones don't excite God. We can all wish—wanting everything imaginable—but it takes time, determination, and hard work to develop potential. Take a look around—it's pretty obvious that women today don't have to work the way previous generations of women worked.

With all of our modern conveniences, we are geared toward a life of ease—sometimes with too much free time. And I think that too much free time sometimes gets us into trouble. In our search for things to do, we often make poor decisions. The bottom line is that many women today have a slightly distorted mentality about work.

A lot of women have wishbone, but . . . they're short on backbone. ☺

I'm not suggesting that we should become workaholics and try to kill ourselves. I've done that myself, and it wasn't good for me. But from that, I learned that we need balance in all areas of our lives. We must learn to regulate and balance the time we spend earning a living, working for the Lord, and enjoying recreational activities or resting and relaxing. We must exercise balance in our finances, our diets, and in every other area of our lives.

The realization of our full potential will only be realized as we discipline ourselves. I am certainly not the only female in Christian leadership today, and I think it would be safe to say that most all Christian women in positions of authority know that in the kingdom of God you cannot say everything you want to say, buy everything you want to buy, eat everything you want to eat, do everything you want to do, or go everywhere you want to go. We must discern by the Spirit what is right and then command our flesh to line up with it whether we like it or not. First Timothy 3:1-10 contains a good description for women who aspire to grow their potential into positions of leadership. Verse ten says, "And let them also be tried and investigated and proved first; then, if they turn out to be above reproach, let them serve."

We are never fulfilled until we become all we can be. Each of us has a destiny, and unless we are pressing toward fulfilling it, we will be frustrated in life. Moving up to the next level requires a decision to press in, to let go of what lies behind and refuse to be mediocre. I believe God wants to do more with your life than you ever imagined. You have a tremendous capacity and potential that needs to be developed. I believe as women of God, we all want to lead something because we have God's Spirit in us—and His Spirit causes us to excel.

I also believe that God is looking for women to promote. You can be one of them. There is potential for greatness in you!

38

Does Anyone Understand Me?

*W*hen women are hurting or frustrated, it seems that one of the things we need most is to know that someone understands what we are going through and how we feel. Just hearing the two words "I understand" can be almost as effective as a tranquilizer in calming a hurting woman.

Because men are wired differently than women, they don't react or respond to situations the same way that women do. Men are more logical and women are more emotional. When we are upset and someone tries to be logical with us, it often only upsets us more. But when someone sincerely says, "I understand," it has a calming and soothing effect.

I spent years getting angry with my husband, Dave, because he never seemed to understand what I was going through or how I felt. As a man, he always offered his logical solution to the problem . . . or worse yet, brought up something from one of my own sermons, neither of which comforted me in the least. Dave loves me very much, and I know that he sincerely wanted to help me—just as I am sure the people in your life want to help you—but he simply saw things from a totally different perspective than I did. His answer to almost every upsetting or disappointing situation has always been, "Cast your care and God will take of it." In theory he was right, but I still needed to get past the emotional crisis at hand.

My marriage improved greatly when I discovered an encouraging Scripture found in Hebrews 4:15, which says, "We do not have a High Priest Who is unable to understand and sympathize and have a shared feeling with our weaknesses and infirmities and liability to the assaults of temptation, but One Who has been tempted in every respect as we are, yet without sinning." What a relief it is to know that Jesus **understands** our weaknesses and infirmities, and because He does, we can "fearlessly and confidently and boldly draw near to the throne of grace . . . " (verse 16).

When I read this Bible passage, I finally understood that I had been going to the wrong person for help when I was hurting!

Quite often we run to people when we should be running to Jesus. It is good for people to comfort one another, but we should always remember that our main source of comfort *must* be The Comforter himself (the Holy Spirit). When we go to God first, He can lead someone to give us what we need, but in essence it is the Holy Spirit working through that person. I believe that God is insulted when we depend on others to give us what He wants to give us.

After I had been enlightened on the matter, I started going to God first—and guess what? Dave became more understanding! God worked through Him, showing him things that I never could have gotten him to understand. If you are a woman who needs someone to understand you, try it. Go to God first when you are hurting or have a need of any kind, and He will comfort you. He may do it Himself or He may work through someone else, but He will see that you are comforted because you placed your faith in Him.

In the Bible we read that Moses expected his brethren to understand that God had called him to deliver them, but they did not understand (see Acts 7:25). Isn't that our testimony also—we expect people to understand, but they don't understand. I can feel Moses' pain in that statement. I can sense his disappointment with people.

When we go to God first, He can lead someone to give us what we need. ☺

We will experience less disappointment with people if we learn to depend on God from the beginning of every situation. I encourage you, my friend, to go to God with everything, because He cares about every little thing that concerns you. He has counted the hairs on your head, and He has all your tears in a bottle. There is nothing that concerns you that does not also concern Him.

Going to God with everything in simple prayer is one of the best ways to develop a deep and intimate personal relationship with Him. Taking your needs to Him also provides an opportunity for you to see Him working in your life as He answers your prayers. Your faith will increase each time you realize that God hears you and cares about everything in your life, both big and small.

Don't be angry with people who don't understand your needs—pray for them. God can teach people in a moment what we could never get them to understand in a thousand years. While you are praying for God to give you what you need, practice understanding others, and you will reap more understanding in your own life. When someone tells you they are hurting, be a woman who understands, and comfort them by saying those magic words, "I understand."

39

Make Up Your Mind!

*W*e women have taken some teasing through the years about our supposed inability to make up our minds. And although we're well aware that it's not a gender-specific problem, I'm sure we are all aware that it is not unusual for the condition of our minds to change.

I'm sure that you have experienced it—one time you may be calm, peaceful, and certain of yourself. Another time you may be anxious, worried, and insecure. You may make a decision about something and be sure about it . . . and then later realize that you're confused and unsure about the very thing you were so clear and certain of only a few moments before.

There have been times in my own life when I have experienced these things. Sometimes I seemed to be able to make a decision easily and stick with it. Then at other times I couldn't seem to arrive at a decision at all. Doubt, fear, and uncertainty haunted me mercilessly. I second-guessed myself and could not make up my mind.

For a long time, I didn't know that I could do anything about my thought life. I thought I was destined to be indecisive. I believed in God—and had for many years—but I'd had no teaching at all about my thought life or about the proper condition for a believer's mind.

I learned that many of my problems with indecision were rooted in wrong thinking patterns. My mind was undisciplined.

Several years ago, I became much more serious about my relationship with the Lord. Through this process, I learned that many of my problems with indecision were rooted in wrong thinking patterns. My mind was undisciplined—it was a mess!

I felt overwhelmed when I began to see how indecisive and insecure I was in my mind. I tried hard to correct the problem by rejecting the wrong thoughts that came into my mind, but they were persistent.

Many women struggle with this because they have spent years allowing their minds to wander. They've never applied the principles of discipline to their thought lives. People who cannot seem to concentrate long enough to make a decision often think there is something wrong with their mind. However, the inability to concentrate and settle on a decision can be the result of years of simply letting the mind do whatever it wants to do.

I struggled with this lack of ability to concentrate for years. When a strong decision was called for in my life, I found that I wasn't confident or disciplined enough to step out and make that choice.

My mind was undisciplined and wandered from the subject at hand. Then I read these important words in Ecclesiastes 5:1: "Give your mind to what you are doing." I had to train my mind through discipline. It was not easy, and sometimes I still have relapses. While trying to complete a project, I will suddenly realize that my mind has just wandered off onto something else that has absolutely nothing to do with the issue at hand. I have not yet arrived at a place of perfect concentration, but at least I understand how important it is not to allow my mind to go wherever it wishes, whenever it desires.

Many times my mind wanders off even during conversations. There are times when my husband, Dave, is talking to me, and I listen for a while—then all of a sudden I realize that I have not heard a thing he's been saying. Why? Because I allowed my mind to wander off onto something else. My body was standing there, apparently listening, but in my mind, I didn't hear a thing.

For many years, when this sort of thing happened, I pretended that I knew exactly what Dave was saying. Now I simply stop and say, "I'm sorry, but can you back up and repeat that? I let my mind wander off, and I didn't hear a thing you said." In this way, I am dealing with the problem. I am disciplining my mind to stay on track. Confronting these issues is the only way to get on the victorious side of them.

Remember, the mind is the battlefield for these daily skirmishes. Indecision and uncertainty are just results of losing these critical battles and can cause you to think there is something wrong with your mind. But the truth is—your mind just needs to be disciplined. Ask God to help you, and then refuse to allow your mind to think about whatever it pleases. Begin today to control your thoughts and to keep your mind on what you're doing. You'll need to practice for a while—breaking old habits and forming new ones always takes time. Discipline is never easy, but it's always worth it in the end. When you win the battle for your mind, you'll be much more certain of yourself—a woman who can make up her mind with confidence.

40

Be a Servant, Not a Martyr!

We all know what a martyr is. We've heard heartrending stories of heroic men and women who, down through the ages, have paid the ultimate price and given their lives for what they believed in. But there's another kind of martyr—one without courage or nobility. I'm sure we all know one—a great and constant sufferer who is always willing to share her pain with anyone who will listen. This martyr wants everyone around to know the sacrifices she is making in life.

I once knew a woman like this. She felt like a slave to her family, and she definitely had the attitude of a martyr. I got very tired of hearing her continually talk about how much she did for everyone and how little anyone appreciated her. I could tell she kept a running account of what she was doing for them versus what they were doing for her. Eventually she succeeded in ruining her marriage and most of her relationships with her children. What a tragedy!

The "martyr trap" is such an easy one to fall into. As women, it's so easy to start out serving our families and friends—and loving it. After all, that's what women do. We always put duty to others before our own ambitions. We are the caretakers, the peacemakers, the ones who assure our family members that we are always there for them and that everything will be all right.

After a while, however, our hearts begin to change, and we begin to expect something in return. After all, we're working so hard and sacrificing so much. Eventually we no longer have the heart of a servant. We become discouraged because our expectations aren't being met. Our attitude sours, and soon we find that we've become mired in self-pity. We've become a martyr. I know—I've been there.

One morning as I got up and went downstairs to make coffee, I felt the Lord impress me to make a fruit salad for my husband, Dave. He loves fruit salad in the morning, and I knew it would be a nice gesture for me to do this for him. He wasn't up yet, and I had time to prepare it so I could surprise him with it when he came downstairs.

The problem was, I didn't want to make him a fruit salad. I could have handled taking him a banana or an apple, but I didn't want to take the time and effort to cut up all the fruit and put it in a bowl and serve it to him. I wanted to pray and read my Bible instead! I thought, *Why do I always have to do this stuff for him? Why doesn't he do things for me? After all, I have to study the Bible and pray. It's my ministry!*

It's funny how we sometimes make the mistake of thinking that spiritual activity somehow takes the place of obedience and makes us more holy—but it doesn't. The Lord patiently reminded me that serving Dave in this way was actually serving Him. So I obediently made the fruit salad and surprised Dave with it when he came downstairs.

I wonder how many marriages could have been saved from the divorce courts if the partners had been willing to show love by serving one another? It seems that everyone today wants to be free—and Jesus has indeed set us free. However, He never intended for that freedom to be used for selfish purposes. Galatians 5:13 says, "You . . . were [indeed] called to freedom; only [do not let your] freedom be an incentive to your flesh and an opportunity or excuse [for selfishness] but through love you should serve one another." This verse confirms that God wants us to be servants.

Words are wonderful, but when we walk in love, our commitment must contain much more than just words. ☺

I definitely love my husband, but sometimes that love is best expressed through service. Words are wonderful, but when we walk in love, our commitment must contain much more than just words. How can I truly love my husband if I never want to do anything for him?

I don't recall getting any particular reward that morning for making Dave's fruit salad. He did thank me, but nothing spectacular occurred as a result of my act of kindness. However, I'm sure that God rewarded me that day with peace and joy and a sense of His manifest Presence. I am sure that He arranged for someone else to do something for me, something that person would not have done had I not sown that seed of obedience.

I'm sure that we women lose a lot of blessings we never even know about simply because we fail to do for others what we would like to have done for us. We always want to be blessed in return from the people we bless, but it doesn't always work that way. We should do what we do as unto the Lord and look to Him for our reward.

If your marriage or family isn't what you would like it to be, you could literally turn it around by adopting this one principle right now. You may have been waiting for your husband to do something for you. Maybe you have even been stubbornly refusing to be the first to make a move. I encourage you to swallow your pride and save your marriage. Stop being a martyr who is always talking about all the sacrifices you make. Begin to serve your husband. Make him the focus, not you. By being obedient to God's call to servanthood, you will reap the benefits of being a wise and victorious woman!

41

Standing Up on the Inside

9 once heard the story of a little boy attending church with his mother and he kept standing up at the wrong times. His mother repeatedly told him to sit down, and finally she got pretty harsh with him about it, telling him emphatically, "Sit down now, or you will be in trouble when we go home!" The little boy looked at her and said, "I'll sit down, but I'm still going to be standing up on the inside."

Have you ever noticed that there is always someone in life trying to get us to sit down? They tell us not to make waves, not to be heard or noticed. They want us to simply go along with the program that others have designed and forget about what we want personally.

Through the years, many people tried to hold me back from the call on my life. There were those who did not understand what I was doing and why I was doing it, so they judged me falsely. At times their criticism and judgment made me want to "sit down" and forget about my vision from God. There were others who were embarrassed by having a "lady preacher" for a friend or relative; they wanted me to "sit down" so their reputations would not be adversely affected. Many rejected me, and the pain of their rejection tempted me to "sit down" and quietly go along with the group.

I had a big God standing up on the inside of me, and "sitting down" wasn't an option for me. $\mathcal{\circ}$

But I had a big God standing up on the inside of me, and "sitting down" wasn't an option for me. He caused me to stand up on the inside and be determined to go forward no matter what others thought, said, or did. It was not always easy, but I learned from my experience that being frustrated and unfulfilled due to being out of the will of God is more difficult than pressing through all the opposition of other people.

Standing up on the inside doesn't mean being rebellious or having an aggressive attitude toward those who don't understand us. It means having a quiet inner confidence that takes us through to the finish line. In Matthew 19:26 (NIV), Jesus shares these encouraging words: "with God all things are possible." Confidence is a knowing inside that despite what is happening outside, everything is going to be all right because God is on the scene, and when He is present nothing is impossible.

If we are to succeed at accomplishing all that God has for us to do, we must keep standing up on the inside and be faithful to God no matter what comes against us. We must never quit or give up.

I believe there are probably very few women who totally succeed at being all they can be. Because the opposition is so great, it is easy to be defeated. However, women who are determined to remain standing up on the inside no matter what happens will accomplish God's plan in their lives.

I challenge you to make up your mind right now to do something great for God. No matter where you started, you can have a great finish. Know what you want out of life . . . what you want to do. Don't be vague! To be confident means to be bold, open, plain, and straightforward—that doesn't sound like a sheepish, fearful individual who is uncertain about everything, does it? Make a decision today to live your life in such a way that you will leave your mark in this world. Decide to be an uncompromisingly righteous woman who is "as bold as a lion" (Proverbs 28:1). Keep "standing up on the inside," and when you depart this world, the effects of the life you've lived will be a reminder to those who remain that you have indeed been here!

42

God Wants to Be Good to You

*D*o you realize how important hope is to our overall health? Women without hope in their lives are destined to be miserable and depressed, feeling as if they are locked in the prison of their past. To get out of that prison and be free to move ahead into a more promising future, they need a key—and that key is hope.

Many years ago I had an extremely negative attitude about my life because of the devastating abuse that had taken place in my past. The result was that I *expected* people to hurt me . . . and they did. I *expected* people to be dishonest . . . and they were. I was afraid to believe that anything good might happen in my life. I had given up hope. I actually thought I was protecting myself from being hurt by not expecting anything good to happen.

When I really began to study the Bible and trust God to restore me, I began to realize that my negative attitudes had to go. I needed to let go of my past and move into the future with hope, faith, and trust in God. I had to get rid of the heaviness of despair, depression, and discouragement. And I did. Once I dug into the truth of what the Bible says about me and about my attitudes toward life, I began to turn my negative thoughts and words into positive ones!

Now, I'm not saying that we can get whatever we want just by thinking about it. God has a perfect plan for each of us, and we can't control Him with our thoughts and words—but we can think and say those things that agree with His will and plan for us.

We can practice being positive in every situation that arises. Even if what is taking place in our lives at the moment seems negative, expect God to bring good out of it, just as He has promised in His Word. You must understand that before your life can change, your attitude must change.

Without hope, women become depressed, discouraged, despondent, and filled with fear. But Psalm 42:5 encourages us to "hope in God and wait expectantly for Him." God wants to be good to you. Lamentations 3:25 assures us that "the Lord is good to those who wait hopefully and expectantly for Him, to those who seek Him [inquire of and for Him and require Him by right of necessity and on the authority of God's word]."

Remember, hope is a powerful spiritual force, but it is only activated through our positive attitudes. And our attitudes have to be based on more than how we feel or what we see around us. Our attitudes must be founded in what we *know* to be true.

Most of us have a hard time believing that God is working on our behalf until we see something happening with our natural eyes, but this usually isn't the way God works. He works behind the scenes much of the time. You must believe that right now He is changing hearts and drawing lonely, hurting people to Him. And right now God is working His good plan for your life—a plan for positive things, not negative, hurtful things.

You must allow faith and hope to operate in your life right now! Without faith and hope, life isn't enjoyable. Every time I fail to apply faith and hope in my life, I stop believing, and I lose my peace—and as soon as I lose my peace, my joy goes with it. No matter what your life has been like until now, you must believe that it can change. Faith and hope are the keys to a brighter, more positive future.

Hope is a powerful spiritual force, but it is only activated through our positive attitudes. ✑

Make a decision to be a *now* woman. God has a good plan for your life *right now*, so start trusting Him today. Believing God brings you peace and rest and puts an end to the torment caused by impatience and anxiety while you're waiting.

No matter how hopeless your situation seems to be or how long it has been that way, I know that you can change because I did. It took time and a strong commitment to maintaining a healthy, positive attitude, but it was worth it. And it will be worth it to you too. Whatever happens, trust in the Lord—He wants to be good to you!

43

Take Off Your Mask

$\mathcal{I}$t seems that many women sometimes struggle to be real. We act one way on the outside, when really, on the inside, we are someone else. Because we have weaknesses, faults, or fears—things about ourselves that we think make us less than perfect or less likable or desirable—we'd rather hide from other people.

Over time, we devise masks in order to more effectively hide these blemishes from others. Some of us devise quite an intricate system of masks to cover up, hide, or give others a different perception of who we really are. In fact, we've become so comfortable wearing these masks that we even forget we have them on.

Our pride, shame, or fear keeps us from taking off our masks and revealing our true selves to others—even those we love. The thought of shedding the layers of deception and defense and standing exposed to the world—so everyone can see our faults, weaknesses, or fears—is simply too much to bear.

The need to be accepted and liked is born in all of us. This desire is so strong in us that we will do almost anything to achieve it. In fact, when we were children, if we felt that we were not being loved or accepted the way we were, we would change. We would completely reinvent ourselves. We would put on a mask or, like a chameleon, change our outer appearance and attitudes so we could fit in better with our surroundings. But inside, that chameleon stays the same—it can't change what it is. The same is

We can change the outside, but no matter how many masks we wear, we can't change who we really are deep down inside. ☺

true of women . . . we can change the outside, but no matter how many masks we wear, we can't change who we really are deep down inside.

The danger of wearing these masks, of course, is that it misrepresents us. What other people see is a lie. It's not who we are . . . who we were born to be. By the time we reach adulthood, we've had years of experience in this type of role-playing and covering up. Our masks have become as comfortable as an old pair of slippers—and we've lost touch with who we really are. We've spent so many years hiding that we've forgotten those things about ourselves that make us different and special.

What a shame! What a waste! Each of us—you, me, and every woman—is uniquely created by a loving Father who rejoices in our individuality. In fact, those distinctive things about us, not our "sameness," make us special to Him.

The little girl with freckles, the young lady with the dimples, the beloved gray-headed grandmother with the sweet smile—they all stand out . . . they're special! And you're special too!

Sure, we all have fears and weaknesses. We're all less than perfect and wish we were better. But you need to know that God loves you just the way you are right now, and His love for you will never diminish. But wait! There's even more good news. Second Corinthians 3:18 says that "all of us, as with unveiled face, [because we] continued to behold [in the Word of God] as in a mirror the glory of the Lord, are constantly being transfigured into His very own image in ever increasing splendor and from one degree of glory to another."

This means that when you believe and cooperate with God's good plan for your life, He will help you to let down the defenses you've had up for so long. God created you, and He knows your fears and weaknesses. He knows how badly you want to fit in . . . to hide your faults and mistakes, but His love is powerful enough to reach beyond all those things and touch your soul. Welcome His touch; feel His acceptance. Trust Him enough to take off your mask and look into the mirror of His Word—there you will find that you are being changed, little by little, into the very image of your Lord!

44

Keep On Keeping On!

Every day thousands of thoughts come to our minds—some good and some bad. But in order for us to be positive and healthy women, we must focus on the good thoughts and let go of the bad ones. But it's always such a temptation to hold on to the bad thoughts. Our minds have had so much practice operating freely that it seems we don't have to use any effort at all to think wrong or negative thoughts. The effort comes in learning to think positive thoughts.

Positive minds produce positive lives, but the opposite is also true—negative minds produce negative lives. Positive thoughts are always full of faith and hope. Negative thoughts are always full of fear and doubt that ultimately can destroy our lives.

It can be very difficult to switch your way of thinking. Some women are afraid to hope because they have been hurt so much in life. They have had so many disappointments that they don't think they can face the pain of another letdown. Therefore, they refuse to hope so they won't be disappointed.

Battles are fought in our minds every day. When we begin to feel that the battle of the mind is just too difficult and we are about to give up, that's when we must choose to resist negative thoughts and determine that we are going to rise above our problems and succeed. We must follow the admonition of Ephesians 4:23, which says, "And be constantly renewed in the spirit of your mind [having a fresh mental and spiritual attitude]." When we renew our minds through the truths in God's Word, He will rejuvenate our minds and give us strength to fight and win the battle for our minds.

No matter how bad the battle rages in your mind, you don't have to give in to it. When you are bombarded with doubts and fears, you can boldly stand and say: "I will never give up! God is on my side, He loves me, and He is helping me! I am going to make it!"

In Galatians 6:9, the apostle Paul encourages us to keep on keeping on: "Let us not lose heart and grow weary and faint in acting nobly and doing right, for in due time and at the appointed season we shall reap, if we do not loosen and relax our courage and faint." Don't be a quitter! Don't have that old "give up" spirit. God is looking for women who will find the courage to rise above all the negatives and pursue the positives.

When the battle seems endless and you think you'll never make it, remember that you are reprogramming a "worldly" mind to think as God thinks. In the same way that computers are programmed, our minds are programmed. From the time we are born, our minds are like computers that have had a lifetime of garbage programmed into them. But God, who is the best "computer programmer" around, is working on us every day to reprogram our minds. As we cooperate with Him and allow Him to help us control our thoughts, He "renews" our minds.

This process of reprogramming or renewing our minds will take place little by little, so don't be discouraged if progress seems slow. Don't get "down" when you have setbacks or bad days. Just get back up, dust yourself off, and start again. When a baby is learning to walk, he falls many, many times before he develops the ability to walk without falling. However, the baby is persistent. He may cry for a while after he falls down, but he always gets right back up and tries again.

God is looking for women who will find the courage to rise above all the negatives and pursue the positives.

Learning to change our thinking works the same way. There will be days when we don't do everything right—days when our thinking is negative. But never stop trying. God is gradually bringing us around to His way of thinking.

Whatever you may be facing or experiencing right now in your life, I encourage you to renew your mind in the Word of God. Then stay positive and refuse to give up! God will be with you, and He will help you make spiritual progress—strengthening and encouraging you to "keep on keeping on" until you press through to victory.

45

Correcting Children Correctly

Being a parent is both a great blessing and a great challenge in many ways. Most people become parents before they are properly prepared for parenting. Sad to say, many parents learn as they go. Mothers who have reared children would probably agree that they made a lot of mistakes and did things they would never do again. I'm sure that many of us who are older and wiser wish we could have a second chance to raise our children.

I personally made many mistakes as a mother, and for a period of time it appeared those mistakes might have caused permanent damage in my relationships with two of our children in particular. Coming from an abusive background myself and still needing emotional healing from my own hurts and wounds, I found myself acting out of frustration many times rather than reacting in a loving way.

As I grew in my relationship with God, I began to realize that although my children needed correction, I hadn't corrected them in a proper way. And with God's help, I learned that if children aren't corrected correctly, more harm can be done than good. Improper correction actually feeds the rebellious tendencies that are in all of us.

As mothers, we must administer discipline with consistent action—not anger. It is important to think about what we are saying to our children and be ready to follow through. Many parents continually threaten, but never act. It takes a child only a short time to realize that Mom and Dad really don't mean what they say. Once this happens, the child ceases to listen.

I yelled a lot when our children were young and made many emotional statements that I had no intention of carrying out. This diminished my children's respect for me in the area of correction. *Don't get out of control trying to bring your children under control!* I'm sure that you, like countless other women, have experienced times when, out of emotional anger, you issued unrealistic chastisement. And later, when you had calmed down, you probably realized that what you said wasn't quite right.

For instance, a mother might say in anger, "You had better be quiet or you will not be going out of this house for a month!" This is an idle threat. She already knows she will not keep that child inside for a month. In this case, the mother is attempting to control the child's behavior with thoughts of outrageous punishment. This mother would be much better off to think it over and suggest something "do-able" before she issues the warning. She might say something like, "I have asked you to be quiet—and if you continue to disobey me, I am going to keep you inside for the rest of the day."

All of us have overheard women trying to control their children at the grocery store. They repeatedly say things like, "If you do that one more time, I am going to take you out to the car and spank you." The only problem is, she never leaves the store with the child to follow through on what she has said she is going to do. She keeps threatening, perhaps each time with a louder and firmer tone of voice, but never follows through with the promised action.

Changing such a pattern is a great challenge, but if you are to gain your child's respect, you must correct with wise, well-thought-out action—not from anger and emotions that are out of control. When we correct our children correctly, the Bible says they will give delight to our hearts (see Proverbs 29:17).

Don't get out of control trying to bring your children under control! ☺

Thank God, I learned to correct my children correctly, and now they truly delight my heart, and we enjoy wonderful relationships.

I believe that proper parenting actually becomes easier when we apply the Golden Rule, doing unto others—including our children—as we would have them do unto us (see Luke 6:31). Speak to your children the way you want other people to speak to you . . . or perhaps the way you wish your parents had spoken to you, but didn't.

Words are very important tools. With them we can bless or curse, build up or tear down. As mothers, we help shape and determine the future of our children, and a large part of this shaping develops as a result of our words.

Never forget to emphasize the great value and potential of your children, and assure them that you love them and only want God's very best for them.

God's Word says that "children are a gift from God; they are his reward" (Psalm 127:3 TLB). So cherish that gift by enjoying your children. Ask God to help you be a wise and godly mother who corrects correctly; whose "children rise up and call her blessed" (Proverbs 31:28).

46

Shake It Off and Step Up!

$\mathcal{D}$o you ever feel that the storms of life are coming at you so fast and furious that you don't know what to do? We all have times when we seem to be bombarded with bad situations—I know that I've had my share! But did you know that there is a right and a wrong way to handle these times of distress? I didn't know that until I became a Christian and began to learn that God's power and peace are available to me. Until that time, I usually got all upset—and many times threw a fit—because things were not going my way.

You may be saying, "Well, how are we supposed to handle them? How can I not get upset when I have problems?" Well, that's the way of the world—that's the way most people feel. But God has a different and much better way for women to handle the challenges of life. He says that we can have peace in the middle of the stormy situations in our lives.

In John 14:27, Jesus says, "Peace I leave with you; My [own] peace I now give and bequeath to you . . . do not let your hearts be troubled, neither let them be afraid. [Stop allowing yourselves to be agitated and disturbed; and do not permit yourselves to be fearful and intimidated and cowardly and unsettled]." And in Luke 10:19, He says that He has given us power. As Christian women, we can have peace even in the middle of bad situations, and we can draw on the divine power of God to help us do what we've never been able to do before.

Think about how awesome it would be to have peace, no matter what happens to you. Stuck in a traffic jam . . . and not get upset?

Get the new checker at the grocery store, when you're already running late . . . and not get upset? Yes, it *is* possible. Instead of losing your peace and getting a headache or upset stomach, you can use the peace and power that God has made available to you and learn to stay steady and calm. This is how you grow spiritually.

It is wise to put that power to work in the little everyday problems and inconveniences that come to all women, because it teaches you to have faith that God will help you handle serious problems—even though they may seem impossible. The most important thing you have to do is to make a decision to believe for the best, and then do what you can to make it happen.

I once heard a story that is a wonderful example of how this works. One day a farmer's donkey fell into a well. The animal cried piteously for hours as the farmer tried to figure out what to do about it. Finally the farmer decided that the animal was too old to justify the efforts it would take to get him out of the well. So he asked his neighbors to help him shovel dirt into the well and end the donkey's life.

As the dirt began falling on the donkey's back, he realized what was happening and cried horribly. (Does that sound like anybody you know—"I just feel like everything is caving in on top of me"?) And then, to everyone's amazement, the donkey quieted down. After shoveling in a little more dirt, the farmer looked down into the well and was astonished at what he saw. With every shovelful of dirt that hit the donkey's back, the donkey was doing something amazing— he was shaking it off and then stepping on top of it. As the farmer and his neighbors continued to shovel dirt into the well, the donkey just kept shaking it off and stepping up! Eventually everyone stood back in amazement as the donkey stepped over the edge of the well and trotted off.

Don't get buried by all the problems that life shovels on you—just stay calm, and keep shaking them off and stepping up. ☺

That's a wonderful lesson about how you can be a woman who wins, even in

seemingly hopeless situations. Don't waste your time whining, crying, or throwing a fit. Instead, calm down and think about the peace
and the power of God that is yours . . . and then put it to work for
you. Don't get buried by all the problems that life shovels on you—
just stay calm, and keep shaking them off and stepping up—and
before long, you'll step out of your problems and walk right into the
victory that God had planned for you all along!

47

Are You As Close to God As You Want to Be?

How close to God are you? How close do you want to be? This is a subject that you may not have given serious thought to before, but it is both interesting and important.

It's obvious that some people are closer to God than others. Some people have a reverent familiarity with God that seems foreign to other Christians. These "close friends" of God share stories of talking to Him as if they know Him personally . . . while skeptical onlookers wonder why they don't feel that kind of closeness.

Why is that? Does God have favorites? Is He a respecter of persons? The answer is no. The Bible teaches that we, not God, determine our own level of intimacy with Him. All of us have been invited to " . . . fearlessly and confidently and boldly draw near to the throne of grace (the throne of God's unmerited favor to us sinners), that we may receive mercy [for our failures] and find grace to help in good time for every need [appropriate help and well-timed help, coming just when we need it]" (Hebrews 4:16). This Scripture indicates that each one of us can be as close to God's throne of grace as we choose to be.

There are various levels of intimacy with God, and each one coincides with the corresponding level of commitment that we have in pursuing a relationship with Him. Not everyone is willing to take the time to develop a close relationship with the Lord. God doesn't ask for *all* of our time. He designed us with a body, a soul, and a spirit, and He knows that taking care of each area requires a certain amount of our time and attention. But as busy women, our goal should be to have proper balance and priorities.

Taking care of our body requires eating properly and exercising. Taking care of our soul includes seeing that our emotional needs are met. Women need to be entertained and have fun, and we need to enjoy fellowship with other people. Likewise, we have a spiritual nature that needs attention, and our spiritual needs are met through a personal, intimate relationship with God. Caring for all these areas requires a commitment of our time.

I believe the whole issue of intimacy with God is a matter of how we choose to spend our time. We say we don't have time to spend with God, yet we take time to do other things that are important to us. "I'm busy" can be an excuse that sometimes indicates that our lives are out of balance. We all have to fight distractions every day to protect our time with God. He is the most important requirement in our lives, so why doesn't He have that place of importance in our time?

Perhaps it's because when we start making a spiritual investment, we want instant gratification. But to seek God means to continue looking for Him. We won't experience instant gratification. We must sow before we reap; we must invest before we get a return. In other words, we must lose before we gain—we must give up time before we can experience intimacy with God.

A commitment to spend time with God is as serious as any commitment that we could ever make. God says in Psalm 27:8, " . . . Seek My face [inquire for and require My presence as your vital need]." This indicates that God is a vital necessity in our lives.

The whole issue of intimacy with God is a matter of how we choose to spend our time. ☺

A person who depends on a pacemaker to correct a heart condition must periodically take time to charge it—it is a vital necessity. That is the way we should view our time with God—as the opportunity to recharge the pacemaker of our heart.

The quality of our lives as women is greatly affected by the time we spend with God, and it should have a place of priority in our schedule. So if you're not as close to God as you'd like to be, the next *move* is yours!

48

It's OK to Lighten Up!

*A*re you anxious . . . tied up in knots, worrying and fretting about things you've done . . . or haven't done? Are you even upset about things that are out of your control? These anxious feelings are common for busy women in today's fast-paced world, but they are not God's plan for our lives. Jesus himself said, "Do not let your hearts be troubled (distressed, agitated) . . . " (John 14:1).

The Bible teaches that this type of anxiety brings heaviness to a person's life. The dictionary defines *anxiety* as " . . . a state of uneasiness; worry . . . abnormal fear that lacks a specific cause." Sometimes this uneasiness is vague—something that can't be easily identified. It is fear or dread that has no specific cause or source.

I went through a period in my life when I experienced this kind of anxiety every day, without even knowing what it was. I was filled with fear and dread for no particular reason. I kept feeling that something terrible was going to happen.

In those days I was like so many other people. It seemed that I was burdened with some unidentified problem that kept me from enjoying life. I was intense about everything—creating problems for myself where none really existed.

Some of the best advice I received . . . was "Stop making a big deal out of nothing." ☺

Some of the best advice I received at that time of my life was "Stop making a big deal out of nothing." I needed to hear that advice because I had a bad habit of making mountains out of molehills. I found myself getting upset over little things that really didn't even matter. I would get so upset that it was a struggle to find any peace or joy in my life at all. I finally just had to learn to let some things go . . . to forget them and go on.

When I began to accept and really believe that God *is* in total control, I no longer worried and stressed out over every little thing. When I would feel myself getting upset over something that really didn't matter, it seemed that God would say, "Calm down and cheer up! Don't be so intense. Lighten up. Enjoy life!" Then I would think, *Oh, that's right. I'm supposed to enjoy life. God is in control!*

As a result of the abuse I suffered while growing up, I was never able to enjoy anything about my life. I never really got to be a kid, so I didn't know how to be happy and childlike. I was so tense and worried all the time that everything seemed burdensome to me. I blew things way out of proportion, making a big deal out of everything.

Eventually God helped me learn that I could relax, lighten up, let things go, and enjoy life regardless of my circumstances. I learned that even if everything didn't always work out exactly as I wanted it to, it wasn't the end of the world.

There seems to be plenty to worry about in today's world, but if we can learn to lighten up a little more, we will discover that it makes the heaviness of anxiety much lighter and easier to deal with. Jesus shares these encouraging words in John 16:33, "In the world you have tribulation and trials and distress and frustration; but be of good cheer . . . for I have overcome the world." The knowledge of that wonderful truth should be reason enough for you to let go of your anxious fretting.

Why not purpose in your heart to eagerly face each new day, saying, "This is the day the Lord has made; [I] will rejoice and be glad in it" (Psalm 118:24 NKJV).

Knowing that God is in control, and that it's OK to lighten up, should make you a much happier woman!

49

Independence—It's Not Always a Good Thing!

*H*ave you ever struggled with your independence? Have you felt the pressure from our society to be a woman who is more independent—less reliant on others? The desire to be independent seems to be deep inside most of us. We set it up as one of our goals in life to be able to make our own decisions and to be our own boss. We don't want to have to answer to anybody or have anyone looking over our shoulder.

This desire for independence is actually a sign of immaturity. A small child thinks he can do anything. Instead of asking for help, he wants to do everything himself. He wants to dress himself, put on his own shoes, and tie his own laces. Often he gets the shoes on the wrong feet, ties the laces together so he trips, and gets his clothes on backward or inside out.

That's the way we are sometimes in our lives. Even though others—our friends, families, and even God—try to help us, we stubbornly refuse the help because we want to do everything ourselves. And many times we just end up making a terrible mess of things.

Once we give ourselves over to God, we must get out of the way and let Him help us manage our lives.

Most of us are surrounded by people who love us and want to help us. Even though they may not always do things the way we would, they really do desire to be a blessing in our lives. Even God himself is always there—waiting to take over the heavy burdens we continue to heap on ourselves. God wants to help us manage our lives. Like any loving father, He wants to help us handle our affairs just because He loves and cares for us. The apostle Peter said, "[Cast] the whole of your care [all your anxieties, all your worries, all your concerns, once and for all] on Him, for He cares for you affectionately and cares about you watchfully" (1 Peter 5:7). But many times we reject His help and try to do things on our own—often with disastrous results. If we want to experience the peace that God desires for each of us, we must learn to cast ourselves and our cares completely into His hands . . . *permanently*.

Instead of giving our cares and burdens over to God completely and letting them remain with Him, many of us go to God in prayer just to get some temporary relief. After a while we wander away and soon find ourselves struggling under the weight of the same old familiar burdens and cares—trying all the while to be more independent.

The only way to really get rid of these burdens is to overcome the temptation to be independent women and place ourselves totally in God's hands.

Once we give ourselves over to God, we must get out of the way and let Him help us manage our lives. We must learn, not to reach back and grab those things that we've given to Him. It's not our job to give guidance, counsel, or direction to God. Our job is to simply trust God with what is going on in our lives, having faith that He will let us know what is best for us.

God is God—and we aren't. As easy as that is to understand, it's hard for women who have been independent to walk it out in our daily lives. We must simply trust ourselves to His care every day, knowing that He is greater than we are in every respect. His thoughts and ways are higher than ours. He has a perspective on our lives that we'll never have . . . but vitally need. If we will yield ourselves and our burdens to Him and give up trying to be so independent, He will teach us His ways and care for us much better than we could ever care for ourselves.

50

Take a Chance on Change

*H*ave you ever known someone who seemed to be trapped in an ongoing and seemingly hopeless situation? They hate life the way it is, but they don't seem to have the necessary determination to break free from it by making positive changes. Perhaps you are a woman who is—or has been—in such a position yourself.

I experienced a time like that in my own life. I had a disappointing and discouraging childhood, full of fear, verbal and sexual abuse, violence, strife, arguing, hatred, bitterness, and resentment. As a young adult, I had so much self-pity that I was miserable. And finally God said to me, "Joyce, you can be pitiful or powerful, but you can't be both. Which do you want?" That was a shocking revelation that forced me to wake up and face the truth. Yes, I had had an abusive childhood and had suffered from all the problems that go with it—but the time had come for me to choose to get over all that and find out what God had planned for my life.

John 10:10 tell us that it is Satan's job to try to steal from us the good life that Jesus died to provide for us. And he works overtime at it—trying to make us feel sorry for ourselves and convince us that we are in a hopeless situation. But John 8:44 tells us that "he is a liar [himself] and the father of lies and of all that is false." If we fall for his lies, it won't be long before we have a totally negative attitude that can cause us to become dis-

> *God said to me,*
> *"Joyce, you can be*
> *pitiful or powerful,*
> *but you can't be both.*
> *Which do you want?"*

couraged and even depressed. He would like to put us in a pit and do everything in his power to keep us there. But he doesn't have enough power to do that when we decide to stand against him in the name of Jesus.

God loves you and His plan for you involves a positive attitude and a good life, but if you are to have it, you must decide to make some changes. As long as you'll let Satan control your life and keep you from enjoying the abundant life that God wants you to have, he will do it—but you don't have to allow it. When you submit yourself to God, He will give you the strength to stand up against the devil. And the Bible says when you resist him, he will flee from you (see James 4:7).

Stand your ground, and let the devil know that you're not going to give in to him. When you take a stand *against* the enemy and stand *on* the Word of God, you'll see wonderful changes taking place in your life. James 4:10 says that God will "lift you up and make your [life] significant." I love that! Jesus will lift you up and make your life worth living.

If you want to be an "abundant life" kind of woman, you must have a living, vital relationship with Jesus Christ, the King of Kings and Lord of Lords. He is alive today, and He wants to live big on the inside of you and make a difference in your life. But if that is to happen, you must be willing to make some changes.

Be determined not to fall prey to self-pity. It is a very destructive, negative emotion that makes us blind to our blessings and the possibilities that are before us. I encourage you to make a decision that you will not waste one more day of your life in self-pity. If you are open to making some changes and doing something good for yourself, God will help you. Be a woman who is willing to take a chance on change, and discover an abundant and victorious life that is far better than you could ever imagine!

51

Keep It Simple!

$\mathcal{I}$n today's busy and complicated world, have you discovered that it is sometimes a challenge to keep things simple? It seems that many women have the innate ability to complicate even the simplest things.

There was a time in my life when I made everything much more complicated than it needed to be. I couldn't even entertain friends without making a huge deal out of it. Once I became a Christian, I began to realize that this area of my life really needed some serious attention. I didn't like complicating things, and yet I kept doing it.

It seemed that my life was so much more complex than the lives of those around me. Every area of my life seemed to be complicated— not only my actions but also my thought processes. I complicated my relationship with God because I had developed a legalistic approach to righteousness. To me, life itself was complicated. I felt that I had a lot of complex problems, and I didn't realize they were that way only because of my complicated approach to life.

When we are complicated inside, then everything else in life seems that way to us.

For example, entertaining friends and guests in our home was

When we are complicated inside, then everything else in life seems that way to us. $\ominus$

something I always wanted to do but never really enjoyed. I could make plans for a simple hamburger and hot dog barbecue with my husband, Dave, and three other couples and, before it was over, turn it into a nightmare.

Many times the act of complicating situations is simply born out of an unhealthy need to impress people. Because I was abused in my childhood, I felt very insecure about myself for many years. People who are insecure try to impress others because they feel they might not be accepted by simply being themselves.

When I entertained, everything had to be perfect—just the right food and drinks, an immaculate house, manicured yard, and spotless lawn furniture. All the children had to look like they just stepped out of a fashion magazine and, of course, I had to wear just the right outfit . . . and every single hair had to be in place.

And because I was afraid someone might feel left out, I would end up inviting several more couples than I had originally planned to invite—which meant there might not be enough lawn chairs outside for everyone. So I would rush out and buy chairs, which we really couldn't afford.

And somewhere along the way, I would decide to change the simple hot dogs and hamburgers, baked beans, and potato chips menu in favor of a more impressive menu. So I would run out and buy steaks that we couldn't afford, and make potato salad that was a two-hour project, and fix enough other side dishes to feed a small army—heaven forbid that we might run out of food and spoil my image! I could have made iced tea, coffee, and lemonade, but I had to have all that plus four kinds of soda pop.

I worked so hard before the event started that I was worn out by the time our guests arrived. Even their arrival did not put an end to my labor. I continued to work most of the time they were there—setting out and putting away food, washing dishes, and cleaning the kitchen.

Then I would feel resentment building in my heart because it seemed that everyone else was having fun and enjoying themselves and leaving all the work for me. By the time the evening was over, I was worn out both physically

> *God finally helped me see that there is no need for me to make a project out of every event in my life.* ☉

and mentally—wondering how a simple get-together had ballooned into such a big deal.

Finally I had to face the truth that my insecurities and my need for perfection were creating the problem. When I sought God's help, I began to understand that in order for me to have a simpler life that I could enjoy, I was going to have to change. Life was not going to change—I had to change.

Does any of this sound familiar? Does it describe your approach to life? Proverbs 16:3 gives good instruction to women like me who tend to complicate everything. It says, "Roll your works upon the Lord [commit and trust them wholly to Him; He will cause your thoughts to become agreeable to His will, and] so shall your plans be established and succeed."

God finally helped me see that there is no need for me to make a project out of every event in my life. Once I knew the reason *why* I always wanted everything to be perfect, I was able to deal with my own insecurities and get into agreement with God. It didn't happen overnight—it was a process, but eventually I was able to relax and start simplifying my life.

If you are a woman who complicates life as I did, you too can roll your complicated works upon the Lord and become agreeable to His will. Life doesn't have to be full of complicated events, so just relax, keep it simple, and let God establish your plans!

52

Surviving the Seasons of Life

*D*o you ever feel that you've reached a certain point in your life that you can't seem to get past? I think most women feel that way from time to time because we forget the importance of the variety and progression of the seasons of our lives.

We are equipped with everything we need to live fruitful, balanced, and successful lives, but we must learn that there are specific things we must do during each season before we finally reap the desired harvest. Ecclesiastes 3:1 says, "To everything there is a season, and a time for every matter or purpose under heaven."

There's a season in life when it's appropriate to suck your thumb, drink milk from a baby bottle, and have someone feed you and dress you—but when that season is over, it's very inappropriate to continue in that manner. I believe all of life is like that—we're letting go of one thing and taking hold of another. We're leaving one level of maturity and moving into another . . . leaving one season and going into another.

When we become mature enough to discern the seasons in our lives, we can get past that feeling of being stuck. ☙

There is a right and a wrong time for every matter under the sun, and when we become mature enough to discern the seasons in our lives, we can get past that feeling of being stuck. Our lives are a progression . . . and if we want to have the fullness of God in our lives, we must plow, plant good seed, and then go through the waiting and weeding season. Only then can we experience the wonderful harvest that God has for our lives.

Plowing is all about preparation in our lives—breaking up the uncultivated ground—turning up things in our lives that we would rather not have to deal with and breaking them into good soil. But when you have asked God to bring change in your life and the plowing starts—don't ever look back. Jesus tells us that "no one who puts his hand to the plow and looks back [to the things behind] is fit for the kingdom of God" (Luke 9:62).

Once the plowing is done, the ground is ready to accept the seeds. I believe seed time represents obedience—learning to do the will of God. Each time we choose God's will instead of our own, we're planting a good seed that will eventually bring a rich harvest.

When the seeds have been planted, there comes a time of waiting and weeding, which can be just as difficult as the other seasons. Most people don't know how to wait well . . . and pulling weeds is no picnic either. This is a time when we must pull out the weeds in our lives—things like anger and bitterness—and unless we pull them out roots and all, they will come right back. Waiting is the time to get rooted and grounded in the love of God, trusting Him to bring the harvest.

Then comes the long-awaited, super-abundant harvest—a time when the desires of our heart become a reality. Our kids change. Prosperity comes. We have favor everywhere we go. We receive promotions and honor . . . and enjoy a season of peace. God brings justice for all the past injustices of our life. Joy is our normal mood. We hear from God and sense and enjoy His presence all the time.

That sounds like a good plan, doesn't it? So if you are a woman who is having difficulty surviving in life, I encourage you to get in sync with the seasons. Follow God's plan of plowing, planting, weeding, and waiting . . . and experience the thrill of a harvest like nothing you've ever seen before!

53

First Place . . . Last Place . . . or Runner-Up?

We women hear a lot today about the importance of prioritizing things in our lives, and in our fast-paced world, we know that's a good idea. If we don't consider how we spend our time and evaluate the significance of the things we consider to be important, it's easy to lose sight of what really counts the most.

God's Word provides a very wise yet simple solution to prioritizing. In Matthew 6:33, we are told that when we seek first the kingdom of God and His righteousness, He will give us everything we need. It is a matter of putting God first in our lives. Simple? Yes. Easy? Not necessarily!

Even though we may feel frustrated with our lives and want God to help, it is sometimes difficult to consistently put Him first. It may seem easy to trust God with your life when you're in church on Sunday morning, but on Monday you may be tempted to take control again. Seeking God and putting Him first requires building an intimate relationship with Him that will sustain you every day of the week. God knows best what women need, and He longs to provide it, but He requires that we make Him top priority in our lives.

Many years ago, when I began my relationship with God, I wasn't real serious about it. Like many other Christians, I put in my church time on Sunday. I was even on the church board, and my husband, Dave, was an elder. The problem was, when I was at home or at work, it was hard to tell the difference between an unbeliever and me. I had accepted Christ, I was on my way to heaven, and I loved God. But I didn't love Him with my *whole* heart—there were many areas of my life that I had not yet surrendered to Him. As a result, I was frustrated, and my life lacked victory and joy.

Finally I cried out to God for help, and thankfully, He heard and answered my prayer. He began to show me that I needed to let Him out of my "Sunday Morning Box" and allow Him into every area of my life.

One of the Scriptures that really bothered me in my "not so serious days of walking with God" was Mark 12:30. Here, Jesus says, "Love the Lord your God with all your heart and with all your soul and with all your mind and with all your strength" (NIV). I used to think this meant that I had to pray, read the Bible, go to church, and listen to Christian teaching tapes from daylight till dark, but that's not true. What it means is that God wants to be included in *everything* we do. Yes, He wants to be a part of our Sunday, but He also wants to be involved in our Monday through Saturday lives as well. He wants to help us in the way we think, talk, and act, and He wants to be a part of every decision we make.

God wants to do great things in the lives of women today, but when we give Him second place, or maybe even last place, we place limitations on what we can receive from Him. We can't have "mainline" blessings if God is a "sideline" in our lives. Putting God first doesn't mean that we become so super-spiritual that we can't enjoy anything. God wants us to enjoy things—He just doesn't want us to be controlled by them. I can tell you from firsthand experience that you *can* serve God with your whole heart and still have a *blast* in life.

> *When we give Him second place, or maybe even last place, we place limitations on what we can receive from Him.* ☺

As you're learning to put God first, there will be times when He'll ask you to do things that you don't *want* to do. But it is in those times—when you're obedient to God, doing what *He* wants—that you're putting Him first and developing godly character. And the rewards are well worth the effort.

So go ahead and give God first place in your life through obedience and fellowship, and experience the happiness and stability that come from a changed life—a life with proper priorities!

54

Be Thankful for What
You Already Have

$\mathcal{I}$'ve come to understand the importance of learning how to live one day at a time. If you are familiar with the stories of the Old Testament, you probably remember how God provided the Israelites in the desert with just enough manna for one day's worth of meals. It provides us with an excellent example of how God thinks. He wants us to live in the now. If our minds are always on yesterday or tomorrow, we're not enjoying today. We need to concentrate on what we're doing now, and enjoy every little aspect of our day today. Why? Because God will give us the grace to deal with tomorrow, but He won't give it to us *until* tomorrow gets here.

Being thankful for what we already have is an important aspect of happiness for a Christian woman living in the now. Philippians 4:6 says, "Be anxious for nothing, but in everything by prayer and supplication with thanksgiving let your requests be made known to God" (NAS). I remember one time when I was praying for God to give me something, and He said to me, "Why should I give you anything else to complain about? If you're not thankful for what you already have, then you're not going to be thankful if I give you more."

You can be happy right now when you learn to live in a perpetual state of thanksgiving and gratitude.

To be very honest with you, I was a little shocked at the time. But the more I thought about it, the more I realized that I had heard the Lord correctly. More than likely, there are some things in your life that God graciously provided in response to your prayers, and you may have been thankful for them in the beginning, but now you're dissatisfied again. No matter what you give your flesh, it just wants more and more. Before God gives me something else, He must be sure that I am mature enough and spiritual enough to take care of it. So we just need to be thankful for what we have and believe that when we're ready, God will trust us with something else.

Good things don't just automatically happen to women when we accept Christ as our Savior. There are certain things we must do— certain ways we must live, certain decisions we must make if we really want to be happy, contented women of God. Too many women are just waiting for something good to happen to them . . . hoping that when it does, they'll be grateful and happy. But you can be happy right now when you learn to live in a perpetual state of thanksgiving and gratitude.

Psalm 144:15 says, "Happy and blessed are the people . . . whose God is the Lord!" It doesn't say, "Happy is the woman whose circumstances are exactly the way she wants them," or "Happy is the wealthy woman," or "Happy is the famous woman." No matter what your circumstances may be, you can make a decision to be happy and content right now. The key is thankfulness.

One of the ways we can show our appreciation for all that God has done for us is to be a blessing to others. When we are reconciled to God through Jesus Christ, we are given the ministry of reconciliation—that through us, through word and deed, other people might be reconciled to God through what they see us do and what they hear us say. The countenance of a Christian woman should be the envy of those around her. What about you would make your friends and family want to be a Christian? Have you ever asked yourself that question?

We should make it our business to affect people with gratitude, happiness, and joy. ◔

We shouldn't go around stealing

people's joy. We should make it our business to *affect* people with gratitude, happiness, and joy. It is how we live our everyday lives that can make a difference for somebody else. We cannot verbally witness to everyone, but our very lives can be witnesses to many people.

We need to stop being selfish and living for ourselves. We should get up every day and purposely be a blessing to somebody. The main theme of our lives as Christian women should be giving, serving, and loving others. Philippians 2:3,4 says, "Let each regard the others as better than and superior to himself [thinking more highly of one another than you do of yourselves]. Let each of you esteem and look upon and be concerned for not [merely] his own interests, but also each for the interests of others."

Unfortunately, many women are more interested in themselves than in any other person. But we are supposed to die to self. Jesus died to self and did the will of the Father, and He ended up with the name that is above every name. And if we will just do what the Lord asks us to do, the rewards will literally chase us down and over-take us!

I have a suggestion, and please take this in the spirit in which I offer it . . . from my heart: Get your mind off your own problems, and let God use you to do something good in the life of someone else. Start right now to sow seeds that will produce a good harvest in your own life. That's what happens when you do good things for other people. If you live that selfless, obedient, thankful life, then God will promote and honor you. He will use you to do things that nobody else could ever do. Be all that you can be and do all that you can do to be a blessing to others. And above all, be thankful for what you already have. God will bless you beyond what you could ever imagine!

55

Five Tips to Help You Live
a Disciplined Life

$\mathcal{I}$ believe that God gives all women a desire and a will to want good things for our lives—so wanting to have a good plan and doing what's right is not our problem. Our problem is exercising discipline and self-control. Isn't it interesting that the fruit of the Spirit isn't God-control but self-control? Proverbs 25:28 shares an important thought about exercising discipline. "He who has no rule over his own spirit is like a city that is broken down and without walls." This tells me that a woman who operates in self-control is pretty powerful!

An undisciplined woman always looks for ways to avoid hard work. Proverbs 31 talks about the ideal woman. There is not a lazy or undisciplined bone in her body! Actually, she's a pretty hard model to live up to—but it's not impossible. This woman is described as being "capable, intelligent, and virtuous" in verse 10. In verse 12, she "comforts, encourages, and does . . . only good as long as there is life in her." Verse 13 describes her as a woman who "works with willing hands." In verse 16, she's a businesswoman who "considers a [new] field before she buys or accepts it [expanding prudently and not courting neglect of her present duties by assuming other duties]; with her savings [of time and strength] she plants fruitful vines in her vineyard."

This is not a lazy woman. I urge you to read the entire chapter without seeing it as an impossible goal to set for yourself. The Proverbs 31 woman submits to God's plan by simply doing it. As women, we need to realize that a disciplined life requires hard work and self-denial, but the rewards are worth the effort.

The Holy Spirit will give you power to control yourself, but I believe there are five things you must do in order to cooperate with Him. First, you need to *get out of denial*—do some serious thinking and admit to yourself the areas where you are having problems. Next, *eliminate excuses*—quit giving all kinds of lame reasons why you act the way you do. Third, *face the truth*—quit hiding from the truth and face it no matter how painful it may be. Fourth, *ask for help*—confess to the Holy Spirit that there are areas in your life that are out of control, and seek His assistance. And last, *stop feeling sorry for yourself*—be determined to start thinking uplifting thoughts and work toward positive, reachable goals.

Begin with things like picking up your clothes, making your bed when you get up, and cleaning the table after you eat. Don't leave messes for someone else to clean up. A disciplined woman doesn't make extra work for other people. Learn to whip hard tasks by getting them out of the way first. And complete what you start. If you get interrupted, force yourself to go back and finish the original task. So many women never get their household chores under control because they start too many projects at once instead of starting and completing one project at a time.

Train yourself to be punctual. Being late is a bad habit that cannot be broken until you realize how rude and selfish it is. When you desire to cultivate punctuality in your life, plan ahead and leave in plenty of time instead of waiting till the last minute and then having the pressure of rushing. A life of constant pressure can cause health problems such as ulcers and high blood pressure. So being on time is not only polite, but it's good for your health!

Stop feeling sorry for yourself—be determined to start thinking uplifting thoughts and work toward positive, reachable goals. ◡

As you start working on your self-control, learn to love your critics. Learn to appreciate the concern and correction of people who care about you—but most of all desire and heed God's correction. Proverbs 1:3 says, "Receive instruction in wise dealing and the discipline of wise thoughtfulness."

A woman who desires to become a mature Christian must learn to live a disciplined life. You must get over thinking that you can't do it because it's too hard. During one particularly painful part of my learning experience, I complained to God about how hard it was. He said, "Joyce, do you want to be pitiful or powerful? The choice is up to you." When I made my choice and asked God to help me, He did. He'll do the same for you.

Disciplined character requires consistently making good choices. Success or failure hinges on the ability to prioritize. So learn to sense what is truly important and subordinate the lesser to the greater. Philippians 1:10 admonishes us to "learn to sense what is vital, and approve and prize what is excellent and of real value."

The fruit of the flesh is no control, but the fruit of the Spirit is discipline and self-control. Allow the Holy Spirit to help you exercise restraint over your thoughts, feelings, desires, and actions. I believe you'll soon discover that you can transform your personal world from frustration to victory through the freedom to be gained by discipline and self-control.

56

Communication Is the Key to Good Relationships

$\mathcal{M}$any Christian couples I know consistently cite an inability to communicate as one of their biggest problems. But the communication issue is not confined to challenges in marriages—it is also a key factor in nearly every relationship I can think of. Understanding the differences in personalities as well as placing value on our differences and making a decision to honor and respect others will greatly improve your communication and, thus, your relationships.

We need to be careful about voice tones and body language. How we sound is very important. It can actually be more important than what we say! I have found that I can disagree with Dave in a tone that insults him, and yet I can say the same thing in another voice tone and it does not bother him at all. Ninety-three percent of communication is said to be nonverbal—68 percent being voice tone, and facial expression or body language accounting for the remaining 25 percent.

Ninety-three percent of communication is said to be nonverbal—68 percent being voice tone, and facial expression or body language accounting for the remaining 25 percent.

As women dealing with our mates, our male supervisors, and other men with whom we work, we need to be aware that men normally respond out of logic and women tend to respond more out of emotion. This is actually the way God created us. It does not make one right and the other wrong, but understanding the difference helps.

Let me illustrate my point by sharing something Dave and I used to deal with on an almost annual basis. I wanted to go on vacation—I felt I needed a change of pace and some time alone with him, so I communicated my feelings to Dave. Since he is not motivated much by feelings, he responded out of logic with something like this: "We can't afford a vacation. We only have a few hundred dollars, and we need a new lawn mower."

His logic did not meet my emotional need, so I felt unloved, misunderstood, unappreciated, and rejected. My lack of understanding Dave's logic—that trying to take a vacation at the time would be a financial pressure—frustrated him. Since he had the role of provider, his logic told him that providing a lawn mower was of greater importance than providing a vacation. His logic saw it as a luxury we couldn't afford just then. My emotions saw it as a definite need. Proper communication between couples who understand their God-given differences and the importance of respect, voice tone, and body language can solve this situation without war.

I felt that I was expressing a need and that my husband should have been willing to meet my need. Dave was and is so great. At the time, he was unable to take me on a vacation, but he invited me to spend a special evening out, which solved my emotional need and kept him financially solvent. Do you see what I am saying here? There is always a way to solve situations if we will stay calm and look for one.

Don't let the devil tell you that it is impossible to be happily married to someone who is different than you are. Make a decision that you are going to try to understand the man or men in your life rather than trying to change them. When you sow understanding, you will reap understanding. When you sow respect, value, and honor, you can expect to reap the same. Genesis 2:24 says, "Therefore a man shall leave his father and his

Make a decision that you are going to try to understand the man or men in your life rather than trying to change them. ☙

mother and shall become united and cleave to his wife, and they shall become one flesh." God's plan is actually glorious if we can stop fighting long enough to see it.

I believe that men and women can actually become one through understanding, value, and honor. We all need each other, and even when we don't agree on everything, we can learn to disagree agreeably. Men have as much right to an opinion as we do. Ask the Holy Ghost to give you a revelation on respect and honor and how to work together as a team. It will literally save you thousands of arguments and turn you into a happier, more contented Christian woman who is loved and admired by those around her.

57

Confront Your Fear with Faith

$\mathcal{M}$any years ago my outlook on life was extremely negative. It was so bad that even up to a few hours before Dave and I got married, I had a lingering feeling that he would back out—that I would show up at the church and he wouldn't be there. I had experienced so many disappointments, devastations, and hurtful situations that I had a mind-set that went something like this, "If I don't expect anything good to happen, then I won't be disappointed when it doesn't." I thought that by thinking this way I was protecting myself from being disappointed, but the truth was I was miserable.

When I first started to study the Word of God seriously, the Lord showed me that I had many deep-rooted fears that needed to be dealt with. One day while I was getting ready to go out, God suddenly made me aware of a strong feeling of fear that was overshadowing me. It was a vague feeling like something bad was going to happen to me that day.

Within moments God revealed to me that I had lived with this feeling for most of my life! So I asked Him what it was. I sensed that the Holy Spirit's answer was "It is *evil forebodings*." I went to the dictionary and found that Webster defines the word *foreboding* as "a sense of impending misfortune or evil." Until this time, I had never heard of such a thing. However, the Lord confirmed this to be true by leading me to Proverbs 15:15, which says, "All the days of the desponding and afflicted are made evil [by anxious thoughts and forebodings], but he who has a glad heart has a continual feast [regardless of circumstances]."

As God showed me this, I began to realize that Satan had been playing the same recording in my ears all my life. It said, "Something bad is going to happen to you." The more I meditated on his message, the more it became embedded in my thinking and my speaking. I received, believed, and spoke his thoughts of fear. As a result, I was in agreement with the enemy of my soul.

I have found that the best antidote for fear is faith. Although we can't do anything to keep the enemy from bringing his thoughts of fear against us, we can choose what we are going to think about. Through the powerful force of our faith and the words of our mouth, we can overcome Satan's attacks.

Faith is a force that draws the will of God into our lives. In order for my fearful mind-sets to be broken, my thinking needed to be renewed. God wanted to deliver me, but in order for me to receive His freedom, I needed to have faith. Hebrews 11:6 says that "without faith it is impossible to please and be satisfactory to [God]."

How about you? Does fear have an active place in your life? I believe that many women experience a myriad of fears, but those who choose to refuse Satan's lies and have faith in God's Word overcome fear and thwart the devil's plan to paralyze them and keep them from becoming the mighty women of God that He planned for them to be.

As for me, once I recognized that fear had an active role in my life, I made a decision to stand against it. Although it made no sense to my mind and I had no emotional *feeling* to back it up, I decided to believe God in order for good things to happen to me. God honored my faith and helped me to develop a positive perspective.

But I sensed that something was still missing. So I went back to God and said, "I don't see that much change in my life even though I did what You told me to do. I have stopped thinking and speaking fearful and negative thoughts, so what's going on?" His response was so clear. He said, "Joyce, you have stopped thinking and

I have found that the best antidote for fear is faith. ☺

speaking fearful and negative thoughts, but you haven't started say-ing positive things."

The Lord taught me that it is not enough to stop doing the wrong thing—we need to start doing the right thing. In this case, the right thing was to begin to speak forth the promises of God that are recorded for everyone to see in His Word. Getting on the attack instead of being under the attack is the key to keeping the devil off our backs.

Genesis chapter 1 tells us that God spoke and created the world and everything in it. Romans 4:17 says we serve a God who "speaks of the nonexistent things that [He has foretold and promised] as if they [already] existed." With this in mind, I made a list of about a hundred confessions—all based on God's Word—that I felt as though He wanted me to start saying. Two and three times a day I began to speak these things over my life.

When God first called me, He put in my heart that I would have a worldwide teaching-tape ministry. At the time I honestly didn't even know what a teaching tape was! So one of the things that I began to say out loud was "I get speaking engagements every day of my life—by mail, by phone, and in person." When I began saying this, I hadn't had a single speaking engagement and had never received an invita-tion to speak anywhere. Now I receive hundreds of invitations every month.

The point is that once I got my heart and mouth into agreement with God's will, God began to move mightily in my life. The more I received, believed, and spoke God's Word against the devil's decep-tive fears, the less Satan was able to manipulate and control me. It didn't take very long for me to begin to see radical changes in virtually every area of my life.

Getting on the attack instead of being under the attack is the key to keeping the devil off our backs. ☺

I encourage you to open your heart to God, and ask Him to show you any area of your life where you are fearful. Fear will attack you, but you are not a coward because it does. Fear only becomes a problem when we receive it and act upon it instead of standing against it and confronting it with the truth of God's Word. The next time fear comes against you, don't say, "I'm afraid . . . I'm afraid . . . I'm afraid . . . ." Instead, open your mouth and say, "Something good is going to happen to me! God has a good plan for my life. Through Christ I am more than a conqueror!" (See Lamentations 3:25, Jeremiah 29:11, Romans 8:37.) When you aggressively stand against Satan's fears, you shut the door on him and open the door to God's blessings.

58

Face Truth and Find Freedom

We live in a world today that is filled with people who are living false lives. These people are always pretending and hiding things from others because they are afraid of facing the truth. They don't understand that truth is a wonderful thing. In fact, Jesus tells us in John 8:31,32, "If you abide in My word, you will know the Truth, and the Truth will set you free."

But as wonderful as truth is, we must be ready to face it. Truth is often harsh; it shocks us into a reality that we may not be prepared for if the timing is not right. Many women live in an unreal world that they have developed to protect themselves.

For example, I had many difficulties in my life, but I blamed all of them on other people and on my circumstances. I had a hard time developing and maintaining good relationships, and I was convinced that all of the people in my life needed to change so we could get along.

One day as I prayed for my husband to change, the Holy Spirit began speaking to my heart. He caused me to realize that I was the main problem, not my husband. That bomb of truth left me devastated emotionally for three days. I was shocked and horrified as the Holy Spirit gently unveiled to me the deception into which I had led myself by believing that everyone else except me was the problem. He revealed to me that I was hard to get along with and impossible to keep happy—and in addition, I was critical, selfish, dominating, controlling,

"The only way out is through." ☺

manipulative, negative, and nagging—and that was just the beginning of the list.

It was extremely difficult for me to face this truth, but as the Holy Spirit—who is referred to in John 16:13 as "the Spirit of Truth"—helped me, it was the beginning of much healing and freedom in my life. Many of the truths that I teach people today came out of that initial revelation of truth about myself in 1976. My life since then has been a series of new freedoms, each one preceded by a new truth.

It is absolutely amazing to realize that all the lies I believed for so many years actually kept me in bondage. I was afraid of the truth, and yet it was the only thing that could set me free.

The only way we ever get free from anything we have experienced in the past is by facing it with God and letting Him walk us out of it. I often say, "The only way *out* is *through*." We would rather find a bypass, but that is usually not God's way. Bypasses are good for road trips but not for the journey of life. In life, the best policy is plain, simple truth—facing everything head on and not bypassing anything.

Women who have become accustomed to avoiding truth may not truly understand what it is and how they can incorporate it into their lives. The words found in Ephesians 4:15 tell us how to do it: " . . . let our lives lovingly express truth [in all things, speaking truly, dealing truly, living truly]." This says it all. Doesn't that sound much better than living a life of lies and pretense?

Don't be afraid of the truth. The Holy Spirit won't call on you to face the truth about yourself until you are ready to handle it. When that time comes, I encourage you to allow Him to lead you out of your fears into a life of blessed peace and freedom from bondage.

Don't be deceived any longer. Welcome truth into your life daily and experience a life of freedom!

59

Playing Hide-and-Seek with God

*T*hroughout my years in ministry, many women have asked me, "Why can't I sense God's presence in my life?" At times I have asked myself that same question.

Some women may wonder if they've done something that caused God to leave them, but that is not the case. In Hebrews 13:5, God Himself said, "I will not in any way fail you nor give you up nor leave you without support . . . [I will] not in any degree leave you helpless nor forsake nor let [you] down." This verse from the Bible makes it pretty clear that God does not abandon us. He is committed to sticking with us and helping us work through our problems.

While it is true that God never leaves us nor forsakes us, He does sometimes "hide" for a while. I like to say that sometimes He plays hide-and-seek with His children. Sometimes He hides from us until eventually, when we miss Him enough, we begin to seek Him. Jesus instructs us in Matthew 7:7, 8, "Ask, and it will be given to you; seek, and you will find; knock, and it will be opened to you. For everyone who asks receives, and he who seeks finds, and to him who knocks it will be opened" (NKJV). This sounds like a good incentive to seek Him—to seek His will and His purpose for our lives.

Thinking about His goodness should cause us to desire a better relationship with Him simply because of who He is, not because of what He can do for us.

Seeking God is central to our walk with Him; it is vital for spiritual progress. Hebrews 11:6 says, "He [God] is the rewarder of those who earnestly and diligently seek Him [out]." This is another great reason to seek Him, but what exactly does it mean to seek God?

One way we seek God is to think about Him. Thinking about His Word, His ways, what He has done for us, how good He is, and how much we love Him prepares us for more direct seeking. Thinking about His goodness should cause us to desire a better relationship with Him simply because of who He is, not because of what He can do for us.

As new Christians, we are very much in need when we begin our relationship with God. He establishes His relationship with us as a loving Father who is always available to meet our needs and to do the things for us that we cannot do without Him. This is good and healthy as a beginning, but the time eventually comes when we must make a transition. We must let go of those beginnings and go on to maturity.

As children are growing up, their parents are happy to take care of them. But as the children grow and mature, the parents want their children to love them because of who they are, not because of what they can do for them. If our grown children only came to see us when they wanted something, it would hurt us. We want our children to visit us because they enjoy being in our presence.

So it is with God. He wants to bless us with all good things, but when we only seek Him for the wrong reason—with the motive of just getting something from Him—it grieves Him. When this happens, He may hide from us for a time. If this happens to you, it's a good time to analyze your motives. Do you only seek God when you need something from Him? Or do you have a longing and desire to truly know Him intimately . . . all the time?

An intimate relationship with the holy God is something to be desired and treasured by all women, and maintaining such a relationship requires our daily attention. When I finally began seeking God on a regular basis, I began enjoying His presence on a regular basis.

So if you're tired of playing hide-and-seek with God, let Him know that you desire to have His presence in your life. As you seek Him regularly, with right motives, He will be pleased, and He will come out of hiding and bless you with His presence.

60

Better or Bitter— the Choice Is Yours!

$\mathcal{I}$f you've ever been used, abused, deceived, misunderstood, forgotten, cheated on, or taken advantage of, you are a woman who knows what it's like to be "burned." Most of us have had some of these painful experiences in our lives at one time or another.

The reality is that there will always be people who irritate us and make us angry—we will never escape every rude, selfish, and unjust person. There will also be times when people whom we've trusted will disappoint us and let us down. Unfortunately, it's almost impossible to be in relationships with people without sometimes getting hurt or offended.

If you've been hurt, you probably know that our first response is usually to get upset or become angry. Having negative emotions when we've been hurt is a natural inclination, and I don't think it is a sin to *feel* negative emotions. I believe sin enters when we begin to *express* these emotions.

I am so grateful that God has provided a way for us to avoid becoming bitter when we've been burned. He has given each of us the power of His Holy Spirit, including the fruit of self-control. Over time, and through experience, God develops in us the ability to control ourselves—to operate in the fruit of self-control while leaning on Him. This means that we don't just say or do whatever we feel.

What is grace? It is the power of God to do with ease what we could never do on our own. ☺

Exercising self-control is a choice—it's *our* part in dealing with negative emotions. But the power to release and forgive the offenses of others only comes from God—we can't do it in our *own* strength. Philippians 2:13 says, "It is God Who is all the while effectually at work in you [energizing and creating in you the power and desire], both to will and to work for His good pleasure and satisfaction and delight."

That's why it is so important to immediately turn to God the moment we are offended and ask Him to give us His *grace* to hold our peace and to forgive our offender.

What is grace? It is the power of God to do with ease what we could never do on our own, regardless of the amount of effort we put forth. "God . . . gives grace [continually] to . . . (those who are humble enough to receive it)" (James 4:6). When people hurt us, God wants us to make the decision to forgive them, lean on Him for His grace, and thank Him for victory throughout the process.

Instead of getting *bitter* about the things we go through, we can recognize these times of testing as opportunities to become *better.* When someone does us wrong, we can take that experience and learn what *not* to do in our relationships with others. Sometimes God uses people in our lives—just like He uses us in the lives of others—to sand off our rough edges.

God doesn't want us to travel through life carrying the weight of the pains of our past. He wants us to be women who enjoy our journey, free of this excess baggage. So I encourage you to be smart enough to stop hurting yourself after someone has hurt you. Make the decision to forgive them, and then immediately lean on God for the grace to do it.

Choose today to let every difficult person and situation you encounter make you a *better* woman instead of a *bitter* one!

> *Instead of getting bitter, we can recognize these times of testing as opportunities to become better.*

61

Smiling Is Serious Business!

*Y*ou are probably aware that there are women all over the world who are dealing with depression—or at least trying to deal with it. There are many underlying causes for depression and a variety of available treatments. Some are effective, but many are not. Some help temporarily . . . but can never permanently remove the torment of depression.

No one is immune from depression or its crippling effects. People from all walks of life—doctors, lawyers, teachers, housewives, teenagers, small children, the elderly, singles, widows and widowers, and even ministers—suffer from depression.

I believe the reason so many people suffer from depression is because they have not learned to deal with the disappointments that are a natural part of everyday life. Everyone on the face of the earth has to deal with disappointment, and disappointment, if allowed to persist, can easily lead to depression.

Disappointment, if not dealt with quickly, can lead beyond depression to despondency and even despair. A depressed person may feel sad and not want to talk to anyone or go anywhere—preferring to be left alone with the ever-present negative thoughts and sour attitudes.

The despondent person, on the other hand, has all the similar symptoms of a depressed person, but the symptoms are much deeper, with dejection of the mind and a failing spirit. The despondent lose all courage, and a feeling of hopelessness quickly leads to despair.

Despair is distinct from despondency in that it is marked by a total loss of hope. While despair is sometimes marked by the abandonment of effort or cessation of action, it can also lead to rage and even violent action.

Recognizing the destructive effects of the process, we must understand the importance of dealing successfully with disappointment and depression in the early stages. The good news is that God can help us deal with it and even overcome it if we just ask for His help.

Once, as I was preparing to speak on depression, I saw very clearly that God has given us His joy to fight depression. Nehemiah 8:10 says, "Be not grieved and depressed, for the joy of the Lord is your strength." As a child, I believe I was robbed of joy. For as long as I can remember, I lived as if I were an adult because everything in my life was so serious. I was brought up in a bad situation, surrounded by negative circumstances.

I thought that if I stayed serious, maybe I could stay alive. Obviously, with this type of attitude, I didn't develop a bubbly, happy kind of personality. I developed a serious attitude—and because of it, people sometimes misunderstood me.

Once I told one of my assistants that I needed to talk to her before she left work. My plan was to ask for her help in making preparations for an upcoming meeting, but because I had approached her so seriously, she thought I was going to reprimand her for something. She thought she was in big trouble!

That incident helped me realize that I had a problem. I knew that my serious demeanor was alienating me from people instead of making me more approachable, so I began asking the Lord how He wanted me to deal with this "seriousness" issue. I really felt that the answer from God was simply to allow the joy that He had put in my heart to show more on my face. God wanted me to smile more!

When the joy in your life is obvious, it rubs off on others. ☺

Everyone knows how to smile. It's one of the greatest gifts God has given us. A smile makes people feel good, and people look so beautiful when they smile. When the joy in your life is obvious, it rubs off on others. But when you keep God's joy locked inside of you and don't allow it to show on your face, you're depriving those around you of a pleasant and refreshing experience.

Most women really don't understand how expressing joy will change their circumstances . . . and perhaps the lives of others—but it does. Living your life with the "joy of the Lord" will chase off negative, depressing circumstances.

I never would have thought that smiling was such a serious matter, but God spent several months trying to get this point across to me. And now I know from personal experience that it's true. I encourage you to start smiling more. Expressing joy through the calm delight of smiling brings good things into your own life and shares the joy and light of the Lord with others.

62

Do It God's Way!

*A*re you a chronic "dieter"? Have you gone on and off more diets in the past than you can count? You are not alone—it is a problem for many women. Thousands and thousands of diets and dieters fail every day.

Most diets fail because they are based on the starvation principle. They deny the body the nourishment it needs to maintain health and vitality. Whenever the body is deprived of its basic requirements, sooner or later it begins to rebel and demand what it needs to perform properly. The result is often the feast and famine cycle—which is why any weight lost is quickly regained.

However, this is not God's way for you to attain and maintain your ideal weight. Yes, God cares about your problems with weight and dieting. In fact, He cares about the problems caused by eating disorders of all kind. First Peter 5:7 says, "He is always thinking about you and watching everything that concerns you" (TLB).

God has a plan for everything in life—including our eating habits! If we really want to maintain proper weight and reap the benefits of good health that go with it, we must eat according to God's plan. There is no other permanent solution—there are only temporary "fixes" that often end in misery and frustration.

God cares about you and He is always available to provide the help and strength you need. ☉

I know of many women who spend large amounts of time and money following various fad diets in a desperate attempt to lose excess weight. Although they may lose for a while, invariably they gain back what they have lost . . . and often even more. It can be a vicious cycle! Others suffer daily with the devastating effects of anorexia, bulimia, or binge eating.

Whatever the reason for our weight problems—whether eating the wrong things, overeating that is out of control, some kind of emotional fear, or psychological or spiritual problems—the underlying reason is still the same. We have been programmed incorrectly when it comes to our eating habits, and we need to be reprogrammed according to God's plan and will for us.

The truth of the matter is that eating right is a matter of great importance if we are to live happy and healthy lives. Eating healthy foods in appropriate amounts is God's plan for all of us. For women who have abused their bodies for long periods of time by not eating properly, changing can be difficult, but God cares about you and He is always available to provide the help and strength you need. He says, "My grace is enough; it's all you need. My strength comes into its own in your weakness" (2 Corinthians 12:9 THE MESSAGE).

This is good news for those who are struggling with being overweight or the problems associated with other eating disorders. I encourage you to go to God and ask Him to strengthen you to do what you have been unsuccessful in accomplishing up to this point. Ask Him to help you change your eating habits by learning to listen to your body about what it really needs and doesn't need. And when you get discouraged and are tempted to fall back into your old destructive habits, run to God for the grace and strength to overcome your weaknesses.

It takes discipline . . . and it's certainly not always easy, but at those difficult times, encourage yourself by declaring: "I can do everything God asks me to do with the help of Christ who gives me the strength and power" (Philippians 4:13 TLB).

By allowing God to help you make right choices about your eating habits, you will be a happy, healthy, and victorious woman. Do it God's way—you'll be glad you did!

63

Be Peaceful on Purpose

Did you know that God wants you to be a peaceful woman? It's true—as God's child, peace is your inheritance. However, that does not mean that you automatically experience and exhibit peace in your life.

Galatians 5:22 lists peace as a fruit of the Holy Spirit. This means that peace must be very important; otherwise, Jesus would not have left it to us.

Jesus had peace, a special kind of peace, and He told us in John 14:27, "Peace I leave with you; My [own] peace I now give and bequeath to you." The word *bequeath* in this verse is a term that is used in the execution of wills. When people die, they usually bequeath, or will, their possessions—especially those things of value—to their loved ones.

In this passage, Jesus was going away. When He passed from this world to go to His Father in heaven, He wanted to make sure that we, His children, inherited the important and valuable gifts we would need to live victorious lives—and included in the gifts He left to us was His peace.

Now, it's not customary to leave junk to the people you love—you leave them the best that you have. So I believe that Jesus considered peace to be one of the most precious and beneficial gifts that He had to give to us.

Verse 27 continues: "Do not let your hearts be troubled, neither let them be afraid. [Stop allowing yourselves to be

Jesus considered peace to be one of the most precious and beneficial gifts that He had to give to us.

agitated and disturbed; and do not permit yourselves to be fearful and intimidated and cowardly and unsettled.]" Jesus says in this verse, "I'm leaving My peace with you, but that doesn't mean that it's just going to automatically operate. It means that I'm giving you something, a reserve that you can draw on, but you're going to have to be peaceful on purpose."

You must understand that the devil tries to set you up to get you upset. He does his best to push you over the edge so you will lose your peace. Why? Because he knows that if you don't remain peaceful, you can't hear from God.

When people lose their peace and get emotional, they start doing all kinds of things that don't make any sense. They may say things they don't mean. They may buy items they don't really want and can't afford. They may eat although they aren't really hungry. People will do all kinds of crazy things when they allow the devil to steal their peace, but it doesn't have to be that way.

God's peace is ours—the Bible says so. That means you can refuse to let negative emotions rule you and not allow others to make you unhappy and steal your peace. When you start to get upset about something, make up your mind to stop it immediately. That is a good place to practice the fruit of self-control. When things start getting out of hand, self-control helps bring the situation back in line.

I encourage you to pursue peace, and be willing to make whatever adjustments are necessary to become a woman of peace. Being peaceful on purpose is an important secret to living the exceptional life that God has planned for you!

64

Are You an Original Classic or a Cheap Imitation?

*H*ave you ever given much thought to this intriguing question? Actually, it is an important question that deserves some thought, especially if you are a woman who feels frustrated, upset, and unfulfilled most of the time.

In today's world, many people are too concerned about "keeping up with the Joneses" or presenting a particular persona. They look at others and decide they should be like them. They set out to make themselves into the kind of person they think they want to be, but too often they discover that it's more than they can handle. Why? Because each person is a unique individual who cannot be forced into the mold of another.

Trying to be like someone else suppresses your God-given right to be yourself, and can cause you to become so confused that you don't know who you are supposed to be. When you reach this point, you are a woman who is in need of a breakthrough—a change that will help you discover who you are and what God's plan is for your life.

I speak about this from personal experience. There was a time in my life when I thought I needed to be like some of the people I admired: my husband, Dave, who is just easygoing, laid-back, and doesn't get upset easily; my pastor's wife, a sweet little, blue-eyed blonde who will sit and listen to someone's problems for hours; and a neighbor who was great at gardening, canning, and sewing—the ultimate housewife.

Those particular qualities were not strong points in my life, but I decided to work hard at developing them. I soon found out that staying calm in any situation—like my husband—was more than I could do. And trying to be like my pastor's sweet little wife and my "super woman" neighbor was too much for me. I quickly became impatient while listening to people share their problems at length. And trying to sew and do gardening and canning just made me miserable.

Attempting to be like only one other person is challenging, but I can tell you that setting out to have the best qualities of three people is impossible. I became so confused and frustrated that I didn't know what I was supposed to do. I was miserable because I was trying to do the impossible instead of what God wanted me to do.

When I finally gave up and asked for God's help, He brought the breakthrough I needed by helping me understand that each person is unique and that not being like everyone else doesn't mean that we are flawed. Romans 12:2 says, "Do not be conformed to this world (this age), [fashioned after and adapted to its external, superficial customs], but be transformed (changed) by the [entire] renewal of your mind [by its new ideals and its new attitude], so that you may prove [for yourselves] what is the good and acceptable and perfect will of God, even the thing which is good and acceptable and perfect [in His sight for you]."

God has given each of us great gifts and talents of our own, but we can't develop those talents if we are constantly comparing ourselves to other people and trying to be like them. If you've been struggling with the feelings of frustration that come with trying to be like someone else, you need a breakthrough—and God wants to help you learn how to succeed at being yourself.

> *God has given each of us great gifts and talents of our own, but we can't develop those talents if we are constantly comparing ourselves to other people.* ☙

So don't be a cheap imitation of someone else—develop your God-given talents and become the original classic that God made you to be. You'll love the difference!

65

Are You Confused?

$\mathcal{I}$s there something happening in your life right now that you do not understand? Perhaps it is your past, and you just don't understand why your life had to be the way it was. You may be saying, "Why me, God? Why couldn't things have been different? Why did things have to turn out the way they did? I just don't understand!"

There are many people today—including women like you—who are suffering from confusion because they cannot understand why certain things happened in their lives.

During my years in ministry, I have discovered that a large number of people suffer tremendously with confusion. I certainly had my share of it in the past, and I know how confusion torments people—so I began to ponder why people get confused and what they could do to prevent it.

As I thought about this, I began to seek the Lord about what causes confusion. As I studied and prayed, I began to understand that confusion comes when we try to figure everything out—when we struggle to find answers for all the questions. That revelation helped me see that it is an effort in futility to try to figure everything out, and I decided that I didn't want to suffer with

[Inasmuch as we] refute arguments and theories and reasonings and every proud and lofty thing that sets itself up against the [true] knowledge of God; and we lead every thought and purpose away captive into the obedience of Christ (2 Corinthians 10:5).

confusion anymore. I still have plenty of things in my life that I don't understand, but there is a major difference now. My faith in God has helped me to stop trying to figure everything out.

If you can just quit trying to figure everything out—which you'll never be able to do anyway—and simply place your faith in God, you will begin to let go of the "Why, God, why?" question, and begin to experience more peace in your life. It almost sounds too easy, doesn't it? But if you really stop and think about it, it does make sense, because all this transpires in the region called "the mind."

The mind is the battlefield where our war with Satan is either won or lost. First Corinthians 14:33 tells us that "God is not the author of confusion" (NKJV), so that means the culprit is Satan. He brings confusion, and then offers theories and reasonings that do not line up with God's Word, which says:

> "For the weapons of our warfare are not physical [weapons of flesh and blood], but they are mighty before God for the overthrow and destruction of strongholds, [inasmuch as we] refute arguments and theories and reasonings and every proud and lofty thing that sets itself up against the [true] knowledge of God; and we lead every thought and purpose away captive into the obedience of Christ (the Messiah, the Anointed One)" (2 Corinthians 10:4,5).

In these verses, the Bible instructs us not to try to figure everything out. When these urges to know all the answers bombard our minds, we need to get control of those thoughts. The Bible says we are in a war—and our warfare, our battle, is largely a mental battle. We are attacked in our minds with confusion.

God wants you to have peace, which is the opposite of confusion. *Confusion* means "all mixed together; unclean; jumbled up; to mistake one thing for another; or to blur." *Peace* means "order; undisturbed, inner contentment; serene." Without peace, it's almost impossible to have joy. And in John 10:10 Jesus said, "The thief comes only in order to steal and kill and destroy. I came that they may have and enjoy life, and have it in abundance (to the full, till it overflows)."

I decided several years ago that I was going to enjoy God and enjoy life. If Jesus died for me so that I could have a full and abundant life—and He did—then I should attempt to enjoy it.

In John 15:1-10, Jesus spoke of the life of abiding, which refers to entering the rest of God. Then in verse 11, He says, "I have told you these things, that My joy and delight may be in you, and that your joy and gladness may be of full measure and complete and overflowing."

It sure sounds like God wants you to be a happy woman who enjoys life. But questioning and confusion will certainly prevent that goal from coming to pass in your life. So I encourage you to make the decision today to live in peace and joy, not confusion or turmoil.

You will need to give up following your impulse to figure everything out and learn to trust God to reveal the answers in His timing. But if you can accomplish this, then I truly believe you will find peace and experience and enjoy the abundant life He provided for you.

66

Learn to Trust God's Perfect Timing

$\mathcal{I}$'m sure that you are like most women—you want good things to happen in your life, but too often you want it now . . . not later. All of us tend to feel that way, but when the good things we desire don't happen in what we consider to be a timely manner, we are tempted to ask, "When, God, when?"

Most of us need to grow in the area of trusting God instead of focusing on the "when" question. If you are not experiencing joy and peace in your life, you're not trusting God. If your mind feels worn out all the time from wondering about God's timing, you are not trusting Him.

The tendency to want to know about everything that's going on can be a detriment to your Christian walk. Sometimes knowing everything can be uncomfortable and can even hurt you. I spent a large part of my life feeling impatient, frustrated, and disappointed because there were things I didn't know. God had to teach me to leave things in His hands. I finally learned to trust the One who knows all things, and I began to accept that some questions may never be answered. We prove our trust in God when we refuse to worry.

> Trusting God often requires not knowing how God is going to accomplish what needs to be done and not knowing when He will do it. ☙

Trusting God often requires not knowing *how* God is going to accomplish what needs to be done and not knowing *when* He will do it. We often say, "God is never late," but generally He isn't early either. He uses times of waiting to stretch our faith in Him, and to bring about change and growth in our lives. We learn to trust God by going through many experiences that require trust. By seeing God's faithfulness over and over, we gradually let go of trusting ourselves and place our trust in Him.

Looking at it this way, it is easy to see how timing plays an important part in learning to trust God. If He did everything we asked for immediately, we would never grow and develop into the women He wants us to be. Timing and trust work side by side.

God gives us hopes and dreams for certain things to happen in our lives, but He doesn't always allow us to see the exact timing of His plan. Although frustrating, not knowing the exact timing is often what "keeps us in the program." There are times when we might give up if we knew how long it was going to take—but when we trust God and accept His timing, we can learn to live in hope and enjoy our lives while God is working on our problems. We know that God's plan for our lives is good, and when we trust ourselves to Him, we can experience total peace and happiness.

It was many years after I received my call from God before I finally began to see major fulfillment of what God had called me to do. God's training period simply requires us to do what He tells us to do when He tells us to do it . . . without questioning.

Proverbs 16:9 says, "We plan the way we want to live, but only God makes us able to live it," and Proverbs 20:24 says, "The very steps we take come from God, otherwise how would we know where we're going" (THE MESSAGE). When God directs our paths, He sometimes leads us in ways that we don't understand . . . and that's okay because He knows what is best.

Our part is to follow the admonition of Proverbs 3:5,6: "Lean on, trust in, and be confident in the Lord with all your heart and mind and do not rely on your own insight or understanding. In all your ways know, recognize, and acknowledge Him, and He will direct and make straight and plain your paths." Most of us have spent our lives trying to take care of ourselves, but when we accept Christ as our Savior, we must learn to trust our lives to His care. When we humble ourselves, saying, "God, I don't know what to do, but I'm trusting You," God gets in gear to help us.

The important thing to remember is that God doesn't do things on our timetable. Yet His Word promises that He will not be late: "But these things I plan won't happen right away. Slowly, steadily, surely, the time approaches when the vision will be fulfilled. If it seems slow, do not despair, for these things will surely come to pass. Just be patient! They will not be overdue a single day!" (Habakkuk 2:3 TLB).

Now, that's good news, so don't get discouraged—just learn to trust in God's perfect timing!

67

Forget the "Ifs" and
Find Your Purpose

$\mathcal{D}$o you have a bad case of the "ifs"? It is a common misconception among many women today that if only we had this, that, or the other, we would find the happiness and fulfillment that we so desperately desire.

Years ago, I thought that was true. I thought that everything would be wonderful *if* I didn't have to work, *if* we had more money, *if* we had a bigger house, *if* we owned our own house, *if* we had two cars . . . *if* . . . *if* . . . *if*. But when these desires were fulfilled, and I still wasn't happy, I realized the problem was something else. So I asked God what was wrong, and He began to show me that I was a shallow, carnal Christian. I was living in the superficial realm of what I wanted, thought, and felt. I was expecting God to give me everything I desired, keep me happy all the time, and always explain to me everything that was going on in my life.

Then the Lord led me to Luke 5—the story of Peter and his companions returning from an unsuccessful fishing trip. After Jesus had finished speaking to the crowds that had gathered by the shore, "He said to Simon (Peter), Put out into the deep [water], and lower your nets for a haul" (verse 4). Well, this got my attention, because I was looking for a *haul* of blessings in

If we want a haul of blessings in our lives, then we need to live on a level deeper than what we want, think, and feel. ⌒

my life. I had Christian tapes, T-shirts, books, bumper stickers, a Jesus pin, and could talk "Christianese" as well as anyone. But I was missing out on the abundant life that the Bible says God wants me to have.

After Jesus told Peter to put out into the deep, Peter said, "Master, we toiled all night [exhaustingly] and caught nothing [in our nets]. But on the ground of Your word, I will lower the nets [again]" (Luke 5:5). Look at what happened in verses six and seven: "And when they had done this, they caught a great number of fish; and as their nets were [at the point of] breaking, they signaled to their partners in the other boat to come and take hold with them. And they came and filled both the boats, so that they began to sink."

Finally I was beginning to understand. If Peter had been living by his feelings, he would not have gone back to fish because he and his men were exhausted. Instead, he chose to live by the word of the Lord. The result of his obedience was an abundant blessing of fish— so many that he had to have help getting them out of the water.

God showed me that the same thing holds true for us. If we want a haul of blessings in our lives, then we need to live on a level deeper than what we want, think, and feel. We need to live according to the *Word* of God and do what it says—whether we feel like it, understand it, want to, or think it's a good idea or not.

We must make a decision to lose the "if" mentality—chasing after things that have no ability to make us happy. It doesn't matter what we have if we don't know and understand our purpose in life— which is to do right and glorify God.

If you desire to be a woman who knows the purpose of God for your life, I encourage you to forget all the "ifs." Untie your boat from the dock and let the wind of the Holy Spirit take you out into the deeper waters of life. Ask the Holy Spirit to help you make the right choices—choices that will bring glory to God and be a blessing to you. There you will experience true satisfaction and fulfillment and come away with a haul of blessings so large that you'll be able to share it with those around you!

68

How to Worry-Proof Your Life

Worry—feeling uneasy or troubled—seems to plague multitudes of women in our world today. It is human nature to be concerned about the bad situations that exist in our world—and in our personal lives—but if we're not careful, the devil will cause us to worry beyond what is reasonable. Worry is like a rocking chair—it is always in motion, but it never gets you anywhere. So why do we struggle with it . . . and what good does it do?

Worry is the opposite of faith, and it steals our peace, wears us out physically, and can even make us sick. Worry is caused by not trusting God to take care of the various situations in our lives. Too often we trust our own abilities, believing that we can figure out how to take care of our own problems. Yet sometimes after all our worry and effort to "go it alone," we come up short—unable to bring about suitable solutions.

At a young age, I discovered firsthand that hurting people hurt people, so I didn't trust others. Therefore, I tried to take care of everything myself, deciding not to depend on anyone who might hurt or disappoint me. Too often it seems that our life experiences force us into this "I'll take care of myself" mode, and even after we become Christians, it takes a long time to overcome it. It is difficult to learn how to trust God, but we eventually must learn that trying to take care of everything ourselves is too big a task.

God will not do for you what you can do yourself. You must do what you can do and then trust God to do what you cannot do.

First Peter 5:6,7 gives us good information about how to change that situation. It says, "Humble yourselves [demote, lower yourselves in your own estimation] under the mighty hand of God, that in due time He may exalt you, casting the whole of your care [all your anxieties, all your worries, all your concerns, once and for all] on Him, for He cares for you affectionately and cares about you watchfully." Since Jesus invites us to cast all of our care and worries on Him, why do so many women refuse to let go? Apparently, we are not yet fed up with being miserable.

The only way to have victory in our lives is to play by God's rules, and He says we must quit worrying if we want to have peace. So when we face situations that cause us to be concerned, we need God's help. How do we get it? We must humble ourselves and cast our cares on Him. That seems pretty clear and simple, yet many women today continue struggling because they are not yet willing to ask for help. But the humble get the help. So if your way isn't working, why not try God's way?

All of us would be better off if we would learn to lean on God and ask for His help. But as long as we try to do everything ourselves, God will let us. He will not take care of our problems and worries— our cares—until we turn loose of them and give them to Him.

Now, casting your care doesn't mean that you are to become an irresponsible woman. God will not do *for* you what you can do yourself. You must do what you can do and then trust God to do what you cannot do. When we humble ourselves and ask for His help, then He is able to release His power in our situations. And it is only then that we can really enjoy life.

When you give your problems to God, you must also decide to be satisfied with His answers. ☺

So the cure for worry is humbling ourselves before God, casting our cares on Him, and trusting Him. Instead of making ourselves miserable trying to figure everything out on our own, God wants us to place our trust in Him and enter into His rest, totally abandoning ourselves to His care. When we learn to trust God, our lives begin to change.

I have learned that my attitude has a lot to do with living a worry-free life. There will always be situations that cause us concern, but with God's help, we can live above all of it and learn to enjoy life. Cast your care on the Lord and say, "God, I trust You, and I'm going to enjoy the life You have given me."

When you give your problems to God, you must also decide to be satisfied with His answers. Trusting God to do what's best for us involves dying to self. Paul said, "It is no longer I who live, but Christ (the Messiah) lives in me; and the life I now live in the body I live by faith in (by adherence to and reliance on and complete trust in) the Son of God, Who loved me and gave Himself up for me" (Galatians 2:20). You can trust God to do what's best for you, so you don't have to worry about it. When you get a positive attitude and keep your faith in God, you cannot be defeated.

If you are a woman who goes around burdened down much of the time, something is wrong. You may have had faith in Christ for salvation, but you haven't moved into walking in faith daily for the abundant, worry-free life that God wants you to enjoy.

The Bible tells us that God is faithful—that's one of His major characteristics. And you can count on Him to come through for you every time. So I encourage you to give yourself—and your worries—to God, and start enjoying a worry-free lifestyle!

69

See Yourself Through God's Eyes

*H*ow do you see yourself? As a Christian woman, your self-image plays a vitally important role in your ability to be happy and successful in life. If you don't see yourself through the eyes of God, you may be suffering from a poor self-image. You may be filled with so much fear, insecurity, and self-doubt that you don't like yourself . . . or anyone else.

I understand that feeling. When I first started walking with the Lord, I had a very poor self-image, and I was very negative about everything and everybody. But God began showing me that not liking myself was the root of many of my other problems. It is almost impossible to have good relationships with other people if we don't have a good relationship with ourselves.

God wants us to have great relationships, but self-rejection and even self-hatred are at the root of many of our relationship problems. In fact, I have found the Bible to be a book about relationships, providing valuable advice about my relationship with God, with other people, and with myself.

Has it ever occurred to you that you have a relationship with yourself? For years I never gave it much thought. Now I realize that I spend more time with myself than with anyone else, and it is vital that I get along well with me. Remember, *you are the one person you never get away from.*

Has it ever occurred to you that you have a relationship with yourself? ☉

Each of us is a rare, one-of-a-kind, precious woman. We each have a God-given destiny to fulfill—a unique calling that only we can accomplish. But in order to reach our full potential, we must learn to accept ourselves as God sees us. Jeremiah 1:5 tells us that God knew and approved of us before we were formed in the womb.

Satan doesn't want you to see yourself as God sees you—that's why he constantly points out your faults, failures, and weaknesses. But 2 Corinthians 5:21 tells us that God sent His Son "who knew no sin to be sin on our behalf, that we might become the righteousness of God in Him" (NASB).

As His child, you should love yourself—not in a selfish, self-centered way that produces a lifestyle of self-indulgence, but in a balanced, godly way that simply affirms the goodness of His creation. You may be flawed by the years and the unfortunate experiences you have gone through, but that doesn't mean you are worthless and good for nothing.

I encourage you to accept yourself in spite of your weaknesses— God does! It is His will for you to be successful in everything you do, but in order to truly succeed, you must have confidence. Not just self-confidence, but God-confidence—an assurance of who you are in Christ Jesus. I think this is a major key to breaking free from a poor self-image and succeeding at fulfilling your destiny.

Over the years, I have learned that the foundation for success is found in knowing who we are in Christ and seeing ourselves as He sees us. Satan would like to keep you from reaching your full potential, but God wants to set you free to be all you can be. So don't settle for second best—put God's love to the test. When you really discover who you are in Christ, and see yourself as He sees you, you'll develop a healthy, balanced self-image and find the confidence you need to be a truly successful woman.

When you really discover who you are in Christ . . . you'll develop a healthy, balanced self-image and find the confidence you need to be a truly successful woman.

Start looking at yourself through God's eyes, and you'll start seeing yourself as someone who is loved and cherished— unique and beautiful in His sight.

70

Live a Healthy Life—
Free from Strife!

God created you and me as containers for righteousness, peace, and joy. Our bodies are not meant for harboring negative things like strife, worry, hatred, bitterness, resentment, unforgiveness, rage, anger, jealousy, or turmoil. We women were built to endure a lot of punishment and still survive, but when we fill our bodies with wrong things for any length of time, we can't escape the damage.

Strife brings stress . . . and stress can eventually bring sickness. Thousands of people are sick today, and every day more and more sicknesses and diseases are discovered. I believe that a lot of these diseases are caused by *dis-ease*—or strife in our lives. The symptoms and sicknesses are real, but many times the root cause is stress and strife. Our bodies eventually break down from so much unrest.

What can help us manage the increasing levels of stress and strife we find in our lives? With all the confusion whirling around us every day, reading and meditating on God's Word centers us. The Bible reminds us of what is important. It helps us to separate reality and imagination. When we base our lives and our decisions on the Bible, peace becomes abundant. It flows like a river. Consider the following Scripture . . .

The wise woman trusts in God rather than worrying. ☺

"Lean on, trust in, and be confident in the Lord with all your heart and mind and do not rely on your own insight or understanding. In all your ways know, recognize, and acknowledge Him, and

He will direct and make straight and plain your paths. Be not wise in your own eyes; reverently fear and worship the Lord and turn [entirely] away from evil. It shall be health to your nerves and sinews, and marrow and moistening to your bones" (Proverbs 3:5-8).

When our mind is calm, our health is protected. The wise woman trusts in God rather than worrying. I spent years reasoning and trying to figure everything out, and it affected my health adversely. I feel much better physically now than I did when I was much younger. Why? I don't worry now. I have learned to turn over my cares to God so that I don't live under the constant pressure of trying to change things over which I have no control.

Learning to turn all my cares over to God has also prevented strife between Dave and me. In the past, I would keep pushing, trying to get Dave to see things my way. Now I back off and ask God to change those things that need to be changed.

I have learned that God wants me to live a healthy life—free from strife—and I've also discovered that it's the only way to live. You too can be a woman who lives a happy and healthy life . . . free of strife!

71

I Think I'm Right,
but I May Be Wrong

*H*ave you ever been absolutely sure that you were right about something? Your mind appeared to have a store of facts and details to prove you were right—but you ended up being wrong. God uses experiences like that to show us how a prideful attitude opens the door to problems in our lives.

Let me give you an example. One evening Dave and I were going to pick up another couple to take them out to dinner. We had only been to their home one time, and it had been quite a while since that first visit. On the way there, Dave turned to me and said, "I don't think I remember how to get there."

"Oh, well, I do!" I promptly told him, and proceeded to give him directions.

"I really don't think that is the right way to go," he said after listening to my directions.

"Dave, you never listen to me," I exclaimed. He knew right away by my response and the tone of my voice that I did not appreciate being challenged by him. At my persistence, he agreed to follow my directions. I told him they lived in a brown house on a cul-de-sac at the end of such-and-such street. As we drove, I gave him directions for all the turns.

As we turned onto the street where I believed their house to be, I noticed a bicycle lying on the sidewalk. "I know this is the right street," I said, "because I remember that bicycle lying there the last time we were here!" I was so convinced I was right that my mind was actually confirming my deception!

Proverbs 16:18 says, "Pride goes before destruction, and a haughty spirit before a fall" (NKJV). Pride and deception always go together—and they were certainly teamed up against me on that evening! We proceeded to the end of the street and—guess what! No brown house! No cul-de-sac! I was as wrong as wrong could be. I slumped down in my seat—completely humiliated.

Has something like that ever happened to you? I'm sure it has happened to all women . . . and probably more than once! Why do we try so desperately to be right about everything? Why is it so difficult for us to be wrong? There are some people who are accused of wrongdoing regularly, yet they never once try to defend themselves. What makes them different from us?

The difference is that they have learned that being wrong doesn't make them bad—they are confident in who they are. They don't have to try to prove anything to anybody. For years I didn't feel good about "who" I was, and in order to feel confident at all, I had to think I was right all the time. I would argue that I was right and go to great extremes to prove it.

Someone was always challenging me, and I lived in frustration as I tried to convince everyone that I knew what I was talking about. The harder I tried, the more problems I encountered and the more humiliation I endured. I didn't realize that arguing over trifling issues to prove I was right just revealed how insecure I was.

As my identity became rooted and grounded in God and what He says about me in the Bible—that I am "the righteousness of God" (2 Corinthians 5:21)—I experienced more and more freedom in this area. I began to understand that my worth and value do not come from appearing to be right in the eyes of others. Feeling comfortable about who I am comes from knowing that God loves me just the

My worth and value do not come from appearing to be right in the eyes of others. ☙

way I am and that He desires a personal relationship with me through Jesus Christ.

When Dave and I find ourselves in disagreements now, God has enabled us to say, "I think I'm right, but I may be wrong." It is absolutely amazing how many arguments we have avoided over the years by using that simple act of humility.

It will work for you too—try it!

72

Which Hat Are You Wearing Today?

The world that we live in today is filled with so many activities that it is difficult for women to keep up with everything. It seems like everywhere we turn there is something or someone who needs our time and attention. However, with only twenty-four hours in a day, there is only so much we can do. That is why it is critical that we establish proper priorities.

Believe me—I know what it's like to have many things pressing in, all clamoring for my attention. I remember a few years ago when my daughter asked me what I was doing, and I said, "Right now I have on my packing-for-the-next-trip hat. This morning I had on my grandmother hat, and this afternoon I need to be a mother to my son. Tonight I will need to wear my wife hat, my niece hat, and my daughter hat because I need to spend time with Dave (my husband) and see my aunt and my mother. Yesterday I had on my boss hat all day, and in a few days I will again be ministering in another conference."

I'm sure that you wear many different hats also—most women today fulfill many different roles. We have many people in our lives who expect a lot of different things from us, and they are all very important. The challenge is to wear the right hat at the right time and to learn when to take off one hat and put on another.

I believe that in order to make the most of everything God has given us, we need to make Him top priority in our lives. Matthew 6:32, 33 says, "Your heavenly Father already knows all your needs, and He will give you all you need from day to day if you live for Him and make the Kingdom of God your primary concern" (NLT).

By asking ourselves some straightforward questions and answering them as honestly as possible, we can discover where God fits in our lives in relation to everything else. I have found that when I put Him first and follow His leading, everything else falls into its proper place.

Many years ago, I was a Christian, but really in name only. My relationship with God was shallow—I really didn't have any ongoing association or connection to Him except through church. I loved God, but I didn't love Him enough to do what He told me—I was just going through the spiritual motions. I had inserted God into my already existing program, hoping that He would make everything in my life work. However, that was not the position He wanted to fill.

God wants to be first in everything. I have found that if I put my marriage before my personal relationship with God, my marriage suffers. The same is true if I put my children and grandchildren before my relationship with God. Although my husband, my children, and my grandchildren are very important, God must be first. If He isn't, I won't have the strength and ability to have and enjoy relationships with them or anyone else.

When establishing priorities, most women tend to forget about leaving time for themselves. The Bible teaches us not to be selfish but to be wise. We must take care of ourselves physically, which includes getting our needed rest. God gave us emotions, and there is nothing wrong with doing things that nourish them. We need to laugh, have enjoyment, and do things that we desire to do. Some women do too much for themselves and others don't do enough. Remember, the key is balance in all things.

Don't allow some small thing that is actually quite insignificant to become a priority that squeezes out things that really should be priorities. Some women, out of their need to feel secure and accepted, get caught up in doing a lot of things for their friends. Those same women sometimes take on too many commitments—they try to

When I put Him first and follow His leading, everything else falls into its proper place.

wear too many hats at one time. After a while, they find themselves running in all directions, constantly feeling stressed, not feeling fulfilled because they are putting their time and effort into someone else's priorities instead of their own.

If you are struggling with the stress that comes from shouldering too many responsibilities, I encourage you to take some time to evaluate your situation. Ask God to help you establish proper priorities by staying focused on Him and fulfilling His will for your life. Remember, all women wear lots of hats, but the challenge is to always remember which ones are most important.

73

Let God Out of the Box

Many years ago, I remember hearing a verse from the Bible for the first time, "You shall love the Lord your God with all your heart and with all your soul and with all your mind (intellect)" (Matthew 22:37). Right away, this Scripture bothered me because I knew that God was not first in my life. But God used this Scripture to create a desire in me to seek a deeper relationship with Him.

It was a learning process—it didn't happen overnight. But gradually, over the years, I began to realize that if I was going to experience any success at all in my life I was going to have to involve God in every part of my life.

I believe that many women today need to understand that if their lives are to be truly fulfilled, they must let God out of the *Sunday morning box*. We must not limit Him to only an hour or an hour and a half of our time on Sunday morning. It's true that He wants to be involved in the spiritual things we do, like reading the Bible and praying, but He also wants to be a part of our everyday activities like washing the dishes, going to the grocery store, transporting children to various activities, and getting the car repaired.

The bottom line is that God is holding everything together. Jesus tells us in Colossians 1:17, "And He Himself existed before all things, and in Him all things consist (cohere, are held together)." The very fact that He is the One who is holding everything together shows how important He is in relation to everything else we attempt to do. Without Him everything would fall apart.

God is concerned about the important role that women fill today, and He wants to help us in everything we do, from fixing our hair in the morning to driving home in traffic. He wants to give us direction in the seemingly small things—from finding a place to park to the larger decisions of choosing a career and finding a mate. God wants us to let Him out of the box and make Him a vital part of everything that goes on in our lives every day of the week, but we have to choose to do it.

With the Lord in the driver's seat of our lives, all our other priorities will begin to fall into place. However, remember, there are no easy formulas. I don't believe that anyone can give us a specific formula for how much time we should spend with God, our families, our jobs, our ministries, and so forth.

I believe that most of us start out following formulas in order to live the Christian life just because it seems easier. But after a while, the formulas fail to satisfy our needs. In fact, I believe that God brings us to the point that He won't give us the energy to simply follow formulas anymore. God wants us to relate directly with Him—not a list of formulas or rules.

I don't have a formula to tell me how many hours a week I need to spend with my husband, Dave. In fact, I don't want a rule that says I need to sit down and talk to him for a certain amount of time each night or on a certain day of the week. I'm not saying this is wrong—I just don't want to live like that. I don't want any "boxes" in my relationship with my husband. If Dave and I need to spend some extra time together, then I want to be able to spend it with him. But at times there may be someone else or another area of my life that needs attention, and I want to have the freedom to devote myself there when such a need arises.

God wants us to relate directly with Him—not a list of formulas or rules. ☉

I believe that God wants women to have the freedom to be led by Him—not by outward rules and regulations. If we are following His leading, He will help us keep our priorities straight and give us the energy to do what He leads us to do. As a result, we will invest our time, money, and abilities in the right way and with the right people.

Remember, only God can help you adjust your lifestyle—but you must first let Him out of the box and include Him in every area of your life. As you allow Him full access to your life, He will enable you to put Him first in your thoughts, conversations, and actions—He will show you how to place Him first in your time, money, relationships, and decision-making.

Don't get discouraged if things don't seem to be progressing as quickly as you'd like. Even though it may not seem like things are changing, they are. My life is a good example of how God turns everything around when we remove all restraints and include Him in every part of our lives. I encourage you to let Him out of whatever box you've put Him in and allow Him to truly be Lord of your life. When you put God first in everything you do, you are destined to be a successful woman!

74

Rejection Protection

*A*re you one of the many women today who are trying to buy protection from rejection?

The pain of rejection is so intense that we often seek to build systems of protection for ourselves—ways to insulate ourselves from its pain. Women construct invisible walls around themselves to prevent others from hurting them. These invisible walls are built in a variety of ways, but here are a few . . .

Inner Vows: Promises we make to protect ourselves such as: "Nobody will ever hurt me again," "I'll never trust anyone again," or "I'll never let anyone get close enough to hurt me again." Initially these things may sound good, but the fact is they place us in a virtual prison. We wall others out, but we also wall ourselves in. We lose the freedom and joy of good relationships through the fear of being hurt.

Pretense: Another protection system we initiate is pretense. When people hurt us, we pretend we don't care and that we don't need them or anyone else anyway.

Self-Defense: We become very defensive, even at times when we're really not even being attacked. A woman with a root of rejection in her life often perceives that she is being rejected when that is not the case at all. The imagination works overtime in the wounded individual.

I have come to realize that I can't buy protection from rejection by trying to please everyone. ☺

Buying Protection: Giving gifts or doing things for people to gain their acceptance and approval. We can also "buy" acceptance or rejection protection through perfection. In other words, we struggle to be the perfect woman, believing that if we can be exactly what everyone wants us to be, they will never reject us because we're perfect.

The word *perfection* means "lacking nothing essential, being in a state of highest excellence. Flawless, exact, complete, faultless, without defect and supremely excellent." This sounds good, but it is not reality. Reality is that we are human beings. Matthew 26:41 says, "The spirit indeed is willing, but the flesh is weak."

As much as I may want to be a perfect wife, a perfect friend, or a perfect minister, I make mistakes. We all do. Our hearts can be perfect, but our performance will never be perfect as long as we are wearing our "earth suits." I long for the time when I'll never have a wrong thought or speak a wrong word. And, oh, how I would love to never have a wrong attitude! But the fact is I don't always reach the goal of 100 percent perfect behavior.

Struggling for perfection to gain acceptance and approval from God or from others is an empty pursuit—God already loves us just as we are—unconditionally. Continuing to strive for perfection only brings us frustration. It may be true that if we could manifest total perfection, we could avoid some rejection—but we will never avoid all of it simply because everyone's standards and expectations are different.

I have come to realize that I can't buy protection from rejection by trying to please everyone. I've laid down my personal struggle to manifest perfection for everyone else, and now I just try to be the best "me" I can be.

How about you? Can you stop the struggle for perfection just to be accepted by others? No matter what you may think about the way others view you, God doesn't reject you! Remember, His love for you is eternal and unconditional and having a vibrant, growing relationship with Him is the only *guaranteed* rejection protection.

75

Don't Trust Your Fickle Feelings!

Are you aware that it is not always wise to listen to your feelings? Feelings are emotions that can change from day to day, hour to hour, and even moment to moment.

Feelings are fickle, yet thousands of women make the mistake of living according to how they feel, often with disastrous results.

I was one of those women for many years—I lived according to my feelings, not realizing that it was the devil playing on my emotions. It seemed that my emotions were constantly going from one extreme to the other—up and down, like riding a roller coaster. I was in bondage to my emotions—up one day, laughing and feeling good, and down the next, crying and feeling sorry for myself. Then I would bounce back for a while, only to turn around and fall right back into misery. (You probably know the routine.)

I reached the point of not wanting to face any type of change in my life because I knew that I was not prepared to handle the various emotional problems it would bring. I finally came to the realization that I was being tormented and controlled by my emotions. I knew that I needed emotional maturity, but I also knew that I needed God's help if I was to attain it.

He was mighty enough to help me overcome my unstable feelings and emotions and lead me by His unchangeable Word and Spirit.

Jesus is often referred to as the Solid Rock. The writer of the book of Hebrews tells us that "Jesus Christ (the Messiah) is [always] the same, yesterday, today, [yes] and forever" (Hebrews 13:8). Jesus did not allow Himself to be moved or led around by His emotions. He was led by the Spirit, not by feelings, even though He was subject to all the same feelings that you and I experience in our daily lives. That means we can count on Him to help us with our struggle for emotional maturity and stability.

Zephaniah 3:17 tells us that the Lord our God who resides within each of us is "mighty." As I sought His help, He assured me that He was mighty enough to help me overcome my unstable feelings and emotions and lead me by His unchangeable Word and Spirit. And He did just that. My life was forever changed. From time to time, I still battle feelings like everyone does, but God has helped me develop enough emotional maturity to know that I don't have to allow my feelings to control my life.

If you have been struggling because you've been believing your feelings instead of believing God, it is time for you to grow up and develop some emotional maturity. It is difficult, and you won't be able to do it on your own, but if you want to be a mature, disciplined, Spirit-controlled woman, "God [who] shows no partiality and is no respecter of persons" (Acts 10:34) will help you learn to walk in the Spirit and not in the flesh . . . just as He helped me.

Ask yourself on a regular basis, "Am I serving the God of the Bible or the god of my feelings?" It is easy to fall into the trap of believing your fickle feelings more than what God says in His Word. And it will take a constant act of your will to choose to do things God's way rather than your own, but when you do, you will quickly discover that life is so much more enjoyable when you are living according to God's plan.

76

Look Up and Learn from the Eagles!

Would you rather be a chicken . . . or an eagle?

That may sound like an unusual question, but it does provide some interesting food for thought about who we are . . . or want to be. One of the main differences between the two birds is that chickens never get very far off the ground and eagles like to fly high. Chickens seem content just to scratch around in a dirty, smelly chicken yard, looking for whatever they can find to eat, but eagles soar high above the ground in the pure, clean air, searching for fresh food.

Far too many of God's children—including women like you—spend their lives "scratching around in the chicken yard," never getting very far off the ground, when they should be fulfilling their destiny and soaring with the eagles. The problem is that many people haven't been taught their rights as believers in Jesus Christ.

If you are a Christian, you are a part of the family of God—and as such, you have access to divine power. But some Christians become bogged down with the problems of life and fail to draw on the strength and power of our heavenly Father. They seem to scratch around in their chicken-yard living, forgetting about their rights as believers. It's a sad thing to see people living in need instead of experiencing their legal rights.

We hear of rich people who live as paupers because they have a fear of losing what they have. When they die, everyone is amazed to discover that although they were thought to be poverty stricken, they were extremely wealthy. They never experienced their legal rights. Fear robbed them, and a lack of proper teaching kept them in bondage. They were somehow deceived, and they failed to benefit from what was rightfully theirs.

Many women who have fallen prey to Satan's deception are doing the same thing—they are settling for less when God wants to give them His very best. Although countless multitudes of people believe in Jesus Christ as Savior, they remain in bondages of all kinds because they really don't understand that God, through His Son, Jesus, provided a much better life for them.

They act just like chickens. They scratch around in the dirt of life with all the other chickens, never getting out of the confines of the chicken yard. But, thank God, there are those who are not satisfied with chicken-yard living. And when they begin to look up, and realize that there are eagles in the sky, they begin to think that just maybe they too can be eagles.

The eagle is the king of birds, the most majestic and powerful winged creature on earth. Eagles are not intimidated by the heights and forceful winds that other birds may fear. Instead, they take advantage of the gales, flying into the wind, setting their wings so the gusts only lift them higher. Nor do eagles waste time battling with other birds that are pests to them. When attacked, they simply mount up higher and higher until they reach an altitude in which their enemies cannot survive.

"Those who wait for the Lord shall change and renew their strength and power; they shall lift their wings and mount up as eagles; they shall run and not be weary, they shall walk and not faint or become tired" *(Isaiah 40:31).*

What a wonderful analogy of the character traits that God wants to develop in His children. We can learn so much from the eagle! No wonder the prophet Isaiah reminds us that "those who wait for the Lord [who expect, look for, and hope in Him] shall change and renew their strength and power; they shall lift their wings and mount up [close to God] as eagles [mount up to the sun]; they shall run and not be weary, they shall walk and not faint or become tired" (Isaiah 40:31).

If you are tired of chicken-yard living, look to the skies and ask God to renew your strength and power so you can *soar with the eagles*!

77

Experience the Presence of God

𝒟id you know that Satan tries everything he can to keep you from spending time with God? It's true! He knows that as women, our lives are filled with many pressing responsibilities that make our days seem far too short, and he uses that to try to convince us that God understands if we don't have time to pray. He knows that if he can keep us from spending time in the presence of God, we will be powerless, unprotected, dissatisfied, and in a constant state of confusion and frustration.

I fell for his deceptions for a while, and I experienced the disappointment of living a powerless and unfulfilled life. Finally, when I was desperate to experience more out of life, I sought the presence of the One who is the giver of live. I discovered that He longed to spend time with me, developing an intimate relationship that would give my life new meaning.

One of the greatest blessings that results from spending time with God is an inward sense of peace, joy, and contentment—a lasting satisfaction that cannot be received from any other source. Unfortunately, there are many women—even Christian women—who try to find fulfillment in a variety of other places. They seek and pursue things, money, promotions, positions, and relationships—trying to gain and maintain their *happiness* based on what is *happening*. I did this for a number of years when I first started walking with the Lord, but when I got tired of a powerless life, I started crying out to God for help.

It was then that God began to teach me that I needed to put Him *first*. He led me to a number of Scriptures, including Psalm 91:1,2, which says, "He who dwells in the secret place of the Most High shall remain stable and fixed under the shadow of the Almighty [Whose Power no foe can withstand]. I will say of the Lord, He is my Refuge and my Fortress, my God; on Him I lean and rely, and in Him I [confidently] trust!" In other words, when we spend time with God, we learn how to dwell in the secret place of His presence. And as we do, we experience an unshakable stability full of peace, power, and protection.

Believe it or not, spending time with God affects *everything* in our lives—opening the door to every good thing we long for in life. Matthew 6:33 says, "Seek (aim at and strive after) first of all His kingdom and His righteousness (His way of doing and being right), and then all these things taken together will be given you besides." When we put God first by spending time in His presence, every area of our lives is positively impacted.

It is important to remember that doing things *for* God does not replace spending time *with* Him. You may serve on four church committees, sing in the choir, and teach a Sunday school class, but none of these activities can take the place of spending time with God. While I was on staff at the church I attended, I worked diligently in ministry for the Lord. I was so proud of myself and all that I was doing . . . until the Lord told me one day, "You work *for* Me, but you don't spend any time *with* Me."

Think of it—God wants to spend time with us. He longs to have an intimate relationship with each one of us. What an awesome opportunity we have to spend time in the very presence of almighty God—but we must not take it lightly. If we are to have a close, intimate relationship with the Father and reap the benefits of being in His presence, we must be willing to regularly schedule some time to be alone with Him.

It is important to remember that doing things for God does not replace spending time with Him. ☙

I have discovered that the best time

for me to spend time with God is first thing in the morning, before I get so distracted with other things that it takes me two or three hours to unwind and calm down enough to hear from Him. I believe this is why the psalmist said, "In the morning You hear my voice, O Lord; in the morning I prepare [a prayer, a sacrifice] for You and watch and wait [for You to speak to my heart]" (Psalm 5:3).

I'm not saying that your time with God must be in the morning, but it is important to give God a portion of the *best* part of your day, not the worst. I believe that as we give God the "first fruits" of our best time instead of our "leftovers," He will multiply our remaining time, so that we can accomplish all that we need to do, and we can do it with joy.

Reading, studying, memorizing, and meditating on Scripture will help us better understand God's character and, at the same time, renew our minds with the truth. By reading the Word, we are actually having fellowship with God, because the Word *is* God (see John 1:1).

Prayer—an important part of spending time with God—is not just about us talking to God—it is also about God talking to us. Once we have spent time in praise and worship to Him and have shared the needs and desires of our hearts, we need to be silent so we can hear Him speak to us. Often He will answer us by reminding us of a Scripture. Sometimes He answers by flooding our soul with peace. But however He chooses to speak to us is up to Him. All we need to do is give Him the *time* and *opportunity* to do so.

God cares about you and He longs to have a more intimate relationship with you, so if you feel the same way, I encourage you to spend time with God every day. There is absolutely no other source that can provide the wisdom, direction, power, protection, joy, and peace that every woman needs. If you long for an intimate relationship with God and a more powerful and meaningful life, it will require an investment of your time. But I can tell you from firsthand experience that the investment pays huge benefits. God loves you dearly and longs to spend time with you today. Don't keep Him waiting!

78

A Cure for the Insecure

Insecurity is a problem that affects a large portion of the world's population today. One article I read described insecurity as a psychological disturbance of epidemic proportions. I believe that thousands of these insecure people are women—some single moms trying to work and find adequate child care and health insurance, others devastated by domestic violence or poverty, widows left alone to face the myriad problems of aging, and wives and mothers just trying to keep up with all their daily responsibilities. With all the issues that women are forced to deal with today, is it any wonder that they are insecure?

So what is the cure for the insecure? The Bible says if your heart is right with God and you reach out to Him for help, "you shall be steadfast and secure; you shall not fear. For you shall forget your misery; you shall remember it as waters that pass away. And [your] life shall be clearer than the noonday and rise above it; though there be darkness, it shall be as the morning. And you shall be secure and feel confident because there is hope; yes, you shall search about you, and you shall take your rest in safety" (Job 11:15-18).

Wow! What encouraging words. Your security doesn't depend on how much money you have, your job, the way you look, how others respond to you, or even how they treat you. Your security cannot be based on your education, your marital status, the label inside your clothing, the car you drive, or what kind of house you live in. Your personal security cannot be in anything other than Jesus Christ and Him alone, for He is the Rock upon which we must stand. Everything else is sinking sand, and it won't hold you up.

There was a time in my life when I was very insecure. I was not rooted and grounded in the love of Christ, even though I was a Christian. In fact, I was even insecure while teaching the Word of God. My security about my preaching was based on how many compliments I received at the end of my services. If I didn't receive enough compliments, I would go home and torment myself . . . sometimes for several days.

I was obviously not rooted and grounded in Christ, although I was preaching and teaching. My security stemmed from the feedback people gave me. Consequently the devil could play games with me and pull strings in my life to bring me torment and insecurity. All he had to do was see to it that I didn't get enough compliments at the conclusion of a service. Then I would be upset because I was depending on the compliments of the people for my security instead of depending on God's approval. I didn't like that insecure feeling, and when I learned that only God is my security, I had a lot more joy.

If you are like I was—a woman who was always looking for something to keep me fixed—you are probably as miserable as I was. But you don't have to be miserable and insecure. When you learn to stand on the Rock, you will find that Jesus is immovable. He's not going anywhere. In Hebrews 13:5, He makes this promise: "[I will] not in any degree leave you helpless nor forsake nor let [you] down (relax My hold on you)!"

The Greek word for *secure* means "having full command." And as Christian women, we have a blood-bought right to have full command in our lives. We cannot be defeated when we trust and rely on Jesus.

If you are a woman who has been tormented with feelings of insecurity, it is time to quit focusing on the people, things, and situations that are making you feel insecure. It is time to focus on Jesus, who is the only lasting cure for insecurity. He took all of your insecurities upon himself at Calvary. His death and resurrection purchased your freedom from the pain and behavior patterns produced by a lifetime of insecurity. So accept that freedom and you will find the cure for the insecure.

When you learn to stand on the Rock, you will find that Jesus is immovable. ☙

79

Listen for the Still, Small Voice

*T*he Word of God contains many promises to the children of God. And I believe that one of the greatest privileges we have as His children is that of reaching into the realm where God is and believing that His promises apply to our individual personal lives.

A large percentage of the prayer requests we receive at Joyce Meyer Ministries come from people asking us to pray that they will know what to do in specific situations—that they will be able to hear and discern the voice of God. Divine guidance is God's will for all His children, but before we can hear from Him, we must *believe* that it is our inherited right to do so.

Jesus said, "All things can be (are possible) to him who believes!" (Mark 9:23). The first thing we need to do then is start *believing* that God desires to speak to us and that we can hear His voice. Isaiah 30:21 says, "Your ears will hear a word behind you, saying, This is the way; walk in it, when you turn to the right hand and when you turn to the left."

One of the ministries of the Holy Spirit is to guide or lead us into God's will for each of our lives. "But when He, the Spirit of Truth (the Truth-giving Spirit) comes, He will guide you into all Truth (the whole, full Truth)" (John 16:13).

As women of God, we can release His plan for us by believing that He will let us know what to do in His perfect timing.

I believe that as women of God, we can release His plan for us by believing that He will let us know what to do in

His perfect timing. We need discernment to do that, not mere head knowledge. First Corinthians 2:14-16 tells us plainly that the natural man does not understand the spiritual man. The Lord used this Scripture to get His point across to me when I was seeking discernment several years ago.

If my spirit brought forth discernment and my head started reasoning whether it made sense or not, I wouldn't make any progress. Why? Because 1 Corinthians 2:14 says the natural man does not understand spiritual things because spiritual things are spiritually discerned. *Your spirit knows things that your head doesn't know!*

Because Satan does not want you to learn how to operate in the spiritual realm, he works hard to bring deception concerning these things. As a result, many people are actually afraid to believe that they can hear from God. They choose to remain in spiritual darkness rather than taking a chance on making a mistake.

I felt this way many years ago when I first discovered that God wanted to guide my life and that I could hear from Him. I felt strongly that He was leading me to do a certain thing, but I was terrified that I might be wrong. I kept asking the Lord, "What if I miss You?" After a few days, I heard the Holy Spirit say in my inner man, "Don't worry, Joyce. If you miss Me, I will find you."

I learned from this experience that because my heart was right—because I genuinely wanted to be in God's will—I could trust Him to lead me. Even if I made a mistake, He would use it to teach me something I needed to learn. As we worked together, I learned to hear from Him.

I don't believe that anyone immediately knows how to be Spirit-led. We need teaching and training. We need practice, and we must risk making a few mistakes.

Making mistakes is not the end of world—but not learning from our mistakes is far more serious. We learn from life's experiences as well as from the Word. Don't be afraid of making a mistake. Be a woman who has a pioneering spirit and is willing to learn.

God speaks in a still, small voice. So I encourage you to make a quality decision to develop habits that are conducive to hearing from Him. Create a quiet, peaceful, gossip-free and strife-free atmosphere, and set apart regular time to fellowship with Him there. He may not always speak what you want to hear, but don't get discouraged. God rarely lets us in on His entire plan at the beginning. Obey step one, and He will give you step two. And always remember to be thankful. Psalm 100:4 says, "Enter into His gates with thanksgiving . . . and into His courts with praise! Be thankful and say so to Him."

I encourage you to follow after peace and obey your conscience. As you do, you will find your sensitivity to God's voice increasing. He *will speak* to you and *you can* hear from Him. Just get quiet and listen.

80

Give Yourself a Break

*D*o you like yourself?

This question may not be as easy to answer as you might think. You may be a woman who is too hard on yourself, believing that you have too many flaws. You may compare yourself to other people and feel that you don't measure up. If that's the case, you're not alone.

Throughout much of my life, I didn't like myself. I didn't realize it, but my self-rejection was causing a lot of unhappiness in me and problems in my relationships. I don't believe I ever would have realized why I was so unhappy—and why my relationships were so problematic—if God hadn't revealed to me through His Word that *I simply didn't like myself!*

Since that day, during my years in ministry, I have been amazed to discover how many women have the same problem. They don't like themselves, and the self-dislike causes all kinds of other problems. They're afraid . . . or insecure . . . or consumed with achieving perfection in hopes of being considered "valuable." They're incredibly shy . . . or obnoxiously bold . . . or they lack confidence in prayer. The list goes on and on . . . and all these problems are rooted in self-rejection.

I'm so thankful that God showed me that no amount of human effort could change a human being. *Only God can change people!*

Let God begin to heal how you feel about yourself. ◌

"And I am convinced and sure of this very thing, that He Who began a good work in you will continue until the day of Jesus Christ [right up to the time of His return], developing [that good work] and perfecting and bringing it to full completion in you" (Philippians 1:6). This verse tells us that we are works in progress!

God doesn't instantaneously change us into someone completely different. He chooses to change us little by little. But during the process, He wants us to know that even though we may not be where we want to be . . . we are not where we used to be! He wants us to recognize that we are making progress. So give yourself a break and say, "I'm OK and I'm on my way!" Start with this basic foundational statement, and from this point forward, let God begin to heal how you feel about yourself.

No matter what you have done in the past . . . or what has been done to you, God loves you. You are the woman He created, and He has assigned enormous value to you. You are an important part—an integral part—of His plan! But it is vital that you have confidence, assurance, and a healthy God-given perspective on yourself.

Don't spend your life being mad and speaking negatively *about* yourself and *to* yourself because you have not "arrived." God is not mad at you because you're not perfect. It is true that God calls Christian women to higher standards and more effective lives—but there is a crucial difference between feeling bad about something you have done and feeling bad about yourself. You may do wrong things—we all do—but that doesn't make you "wrong altogether" as a child of God.

I encourage you to make a decision to *accept yourself where you are,* knowing that God is working in you continuously, making healthy changes and positive adjustments. Begin to get God's perspective on yourself—and God's perspective is that you are OK . . . and you are on your way to the wonderful fulfillment of His ideal plan for your life!

81

Make Way for a New Beginning

*D*o you ever feel stuck in one place in your life? Do you feel anchored to the past—unable to take any positive steps forward? In order to move ahead and make a fresh start, you must be a woman who is not afraid to step out and actually make a way for a new beginning.

Before we can take these positive first steps forward, it's vital that we develop a fresh new view of the way God sees us. God does not withhold His love, acceptance, and assistance from us because we fail from time to time. He is not looking for a perfect performance—just a willing heart that is surrendered to Him.

God gave me a good example of this many years ago. My husband, Dave, and I needed a way to help motivate our youngest son, Danny, to keep his room clean and do a few chores around the house. We devised a chart with a system of check marks and stars. Every time he did what was required of him, we gave him a check. After he had earned a certain number of checks, we gave him a star. And after he had earned a certain number of stars, we bought him a present. Sometimes he had plenty of checks and stars, and other times he had very few.

Every day God gives you the opportunity for a fresh start with a clean slate. ☙

During that period of time, there was a bully in our neighborhood who was always taking Danny's ball away from him. Every time this bully would aggravate Danny, he would come running to the garage, screaming, "Daddy!" Dave would nearly tear the door off its hinges in order to get outside to protect him.

One day following one of these incidents, I was reminded of my relationship with God. I wondered what kind of parents we would be if, every time Danny came screaming for help because of that bully, we went to his room to see how many check marks and stars he had before we rescued him? We would be pitiful parents if we only protected him when he did everything right.

This example really opened my eyes—it gave me a whole new perspective on how God sees us. A system of checks and stars may work with our children, but God doesn't do that with us. He doesn't give us a check mark for every chapter of the Bible we read or for every time we pray or go to church. When we become challenged by the circumstances of life and reach out to God for help, He doesn't look first to see if we've "done all our chores." When we cry out to Him, He steps in and helps us just because we are His children.

Now, God does not close His eyes to our sin. If we do something wrong or get out of line—there are consequences, and He will correct us. However, He would never refuse to help us just because we don't have enough "points."

God has a plan—a new beginning—for each of us. In order for us to see this promise become a reality, we must choose to look away from the past and look forward to what God wants to do in our lives. He wants us to stop looking at where we are, where we've been, and what we've done. He wants us to look from where we are to where we're headed.

No matter how deep the pit you are in, God's arm is not too short to reach down and pull you out. If you have made mistakes, get right with God and go on. Every day God gives you the opportunity for a fresh start with a clean slate.

Begin to see yourself the way God sees you—as one of His dear children. Get your mind off the past. Open your eyes up to what God wants to do in you today. In Him there are no dead ends—only places for new beginnings!

ABOUT THE AUTHOR

JOYCE MEYER is one of the world's leading practical Bible teachers. A #1 *New York Times* bestselling author, she has written more than seventy inspirational books, including *Look Great, Feel Great*, the entire Battlefield of the Mind family of books, and many others. She has also released thousands of audio teachings as well as a complete video library. Joyce's *Enjoying Everyday Life*® radio and television programs are broadcast around the world, and she travels extensively conducting conferences. Joyce and her husband, Dave, are the parents of four grown children and make their home in St. Louis, Missouri.

To contact the author in the United States:
Joyce Meyer Ministries
P.O. Box 655
Fenton, Missouri 63026
(636) 349-0303
www.joycemeyer.org

Please include your testimony or help received from this book when you write. Your prayer requests are welcome.

To contact the author in Canada:
Joyce Meyer Ministries Canada, Inc.
Lambeth Box 1300
London, ON N6P 1T5
(636) 349-0303

To contact the author in Australia:
Joyce Meyer Ministries-Australia
Locked Bag 77
Mansfield Delivery Centre
Queensland 4122
07 3349 1200

To contact the author in England:
Joyce Meyer Ministries
P.O. Box 1549
Windsor
SL4 1GT
Great Britain
(0) 1753-831102

Other Books by Joyce Meyer

Battlefield of the Mind*
Battlefield of the Mind Devotional
Approval Addiction
Ending Your Day Right
In Pursuit of Peace
The Secret Power of Speaking God's Word
Seven Things That Steal Your Joy
Starting Your Day Right
Beauty for Ashes Revised Edition
How to Hear from God*
Knowing God Intimately
The Power of Forgiveness
The Power of Determination
The Power of Being Positive
The Secrets of Spiritual Power
The Battle Belongs to the Lord
The Secrets of Exceptional Living
Eight Ways to Keep the Devil Under Your Feet
Teenagers Are People Too!
Filled with the Spirit
Celebration of Simplicity
The Joy of Believing Prayer
Never Lose Heart
Being the Person God Made You to Be
A Leader in the Making
"Good Morning, This Is God!"
Jesus—Name Above All Names
Making Marriage Work
(*Previously published as* Help Me—I'm Married!)
Reduce Me to Love
Be Healed in Jesus' Name
How to Succeed at Being Yourself

Weary Warriors, Faiting Saints
Life in the Word Devotional
Be Anxious for Nothing*
Straight Talk Omnibus
Don't Dread
Managing Your Emotions
Healing the Brokenhearted
Me and My Big Mouth!*
Prepare to Prosper
Do It Afraid!
Expect a Move of God in Your Life . . . Suddenly!
Enjoying Where You Are on the Way to Where You Are Going
The Most Important Decision You Will Ever Make
When, God, When?
Why, God, Why?
The Word, the Name, the Blood
Tell Them I Love Them
Peace
The Root of Rejection
If Not for the Grace of God*

Joyce Meyer Spanish Titles

Las Siete Cosas Que Te Roban el Gozo
(Seven Things That Steal Your Joy)
Empezando Tu Dia Bien (Starting Your Day Right)

*Study Guide available for this title

Books by Dave Meyer

Life Lines